Work-Life Balance Doesn't Work

How to Create Happiness and Well-Being in 5 Steps

Ignacio Segovia

Worklifebalancedoesntwork.com

Work-Life Balance Doesn't Work: How to Create Happiness and Well-Being in 5 Steps

Ignacio Segovia

Disclosure: This book is not meant to cure any mental disorder. The author of this book presents this information as a business/life coach who aims to help individuals discover happiness and well-being in their lives. If you're suffering from a psychological or psychiatric issue, please seek professional support.

Publisher: Ignacio Jose Segovia
330 Rue Avro
Pointe-Claire, QC, H9R 5W5, Canada.

www.ignaciosegovia.com

www.worklifebalancedoesntwork.com

Ignacio Segovia is available to speak at your business or conference event on a variety of topics.

For booking information, schedule a call at

https://swiy.co/calendar

Why Read This Book

There's no easier way to make dramatic changes in your life than recognizing where you are and where you want to be. Almost every major book on personal development, from Napoleon Hill's *Think and Grow Rich* to Jordan B. Peterson's *12 Rules for Life*, emphasizes the importance of self-awareness for a full life well lived. This book explains how to get the most out of life by learning how to master self-awareness in only five simple steps.

Self-awareness appears to be a mystery to most people, yet it may be easily achieved by children! Hundreds of academic studies have confirmed the effectiveness of taking personal responsibility and leadership in any area of life in treating mental issues, modifying habits, and gaining emotional control. It has the ability to make you rich as well. In some ways, this book will pay for itself through your success. This easy five-step process can assist you in overcoming difficulties, being more creative, and starting a new chapter in your life.

Are you ready to make a difference in your life?

Do you want to make these improvements feel permanent and important?

This book presents the evidence and then guides you through methods based on research in a straightforward step-by-step structure, ensuring that you take the actions you need to make changes at your own speed and with confidence.

Written by a leading expert with eighteen years of experience in organizational psychology, individual psychotherapy, and coaching.

Get more tools on our website to help you take action on your unique personal objectives!
www.worklifebalancedoesntwork.com

About the Author

Ignacio Segovia is a psychologist, coach, hypnotist, writer, and lecturer. He holds a bachelor's degree in psychology from the Central University of Venezuela and a master's in industrial-organizational psychology and ergonomics from Paris Nanterre University in France. He is certified as a professional hypnotist and hypnosis instructor by the International Certification Board of Clinical Hypnotherapy. In Canada, Ignacio studied industrial security at Ryerson University, human resources management at Humber College, social work at Sheridan College, and small business entrepreneurship at Niagara College. His experience as an ergonomics consultant in companies such as PepsiCo, Frito-Lay, Cargill, Global Glass, and ConocoPhillips; his role in small business development under the mentorship of Paul Morgan (Plan2Profit); and his years as a psychotherapist under the supervision of Dr. Dan Dalton provide Ignacio Segovia with all the tools to equip you with solutions in many areas.

Do you want Ignacio J. Segovia to be the motivational speaker at your next event? Request an appointment on his calendar;

https://swiy.co/calendar

Get more tools on our website to help you take action on your unique personal objectives!
www.worklifebalancedoesntwork.com

What Others Are Saying About This Book

"In his book, Ignacio provides incredible and much-needed 'life solutions' to the world we live in today with so many changes happening around us. He helps us live happy and efficient lives not only through his teachings but also through his own life experiences. As Ignacio explains, 'Magic will appear when you are ready,' and I assure you it will if you follow his guidance. He prepares you for it through the steps this amazing book details. If you commit and stay open to the valuable five steps Ignacio shares, you will transition from your old paradigm to a new one full of events that will surprise you."

Paola Valencia, Global Tender
Management and Compliance, Client

"Ignacio explores one of the most important topics anyone can consider; how to get this life right. More than exploring, he gives you a step-by-step process to find the happiness that eludes so many people. If you are seeking a road map to a fulfilling and meaningful life, you need look no further."

Joshua Cadillac, Residential & Commercial
Real Estate Sales Expert and Trainer

"In his newest book, author and hypnotist Ignacio Segovia will lead you through a step-by-step analysis to find your path to a happier, more successful life. He himself is living proof that you can make dynamic changes in your life. Where are you now? Where do you want to be? Let Ignacio help you answer these questions and reach your goals."

Jayne M. Wesler, Psycotherapist,
Attorney, Author, Coach & Speaker

"Have unresolved challenges from your past spilled over into your present life? Do not feel overwhelmed or defeated. Use Ignacio Segovia's 5-Step Method as your map for making change and creating positive foundations for your life."

Silvia Alf, College Literature Professor

"This book begins with the author's personal experience with depression and shows how you are not alone in this kind of journey. Famous figures such as The Rock and Robin Williams are cited in this book to demonstrate that the work-balance life is a fallacy that we have grown up with but DOES NOT produce a happy life. In this book, Ignacio Segovia provides a very logical path to truly achieving happiness and well-being to keep your life in +5 style or as close to it as you can get. Thank you, Ignacio, for bringing to light the fact that you need to know and work on yourself to find your own meaning and happiness."

Zuheymar Brazon, EC-4
Bilingual Generalist Teacheor

"This book gives great knowledge that can help you in your day-to-day life. It also gives you the tools to move forward and live a happy life."

Alejandro Duarte, CEO at
Alewho IT Solutions, Client

"A wonderful modern approach to positive psychology. Very easy, personable reading that speaks directly to people ready to make a change in their lives. If you are an immigrant dealing with many adversities and trying to fit in or struggling with the radical social changes of this era or social media pressure or life challenges, this book will show you that you are not alone and there are ways to thrive and move toward a much more satisfying stage of life."

Isabel Brazon, Director of
Baila Baila, Songwriter and Singer

Table of Contents

Work-Life Balance Doesn't Work

How to Achieve Happiness and Well-Being in 5 Steps

Your life isn't simply a collection of Instagram photos. A wonderful happy moment may happen to you sometimes, but it's an exception. Life's how your children greet you at the door after coming home from work every day (ten minutes each day). It's how you interact with one another over dinner (ninety minutes every day).

If you can, get those basic tasks right, those things you do every day, things that bring happiness, well-being, and success daily, then put them all together as one. You will notice they are not minor; they represent a substantial amount of your life's content. Change those moments, and you will change your life.

Hello, my name is Ignacio Segovia "The *Ergon*."
Ignacio means "fiery one."
Segovia means "the path to victory."
If you allow me, I can be your fiery friend on your path to victory.

Chapter 1 | Installing the WEB

The Rocks from the earth also need help with mental health.

"I found that with depression, one of the most important things you can realize is that you're not alone. You're not the first to go through it. You're not gonna be the last to go through it." — Dwayne "The Rock" Johnson

This meeting room is dark at night. The only light is the moon's reflection on the white snow outside. During the day, it's full of smiles. However, now, this once social place is dark. Full of sadness and tears. This conference room is; the place of refuge from bullies, harassment, and hypocrisy; the place where a grown man can express his emotions, his pain, his fear, his frustration. And I know it is not only me. Yesterday one of the guys at the warehouse approached me and said: "You are not the only one who feels this way. I have been praying too. I cannot believe the kind of people we have to deal with in here. I am sick of it, and I ask our Lord to help. I beg Him to have mercy on these people who mistreat us."

He tried to hide it, but I saw it. A tear rolled down his cheek before he left.

However, the only thing I can see in this dark room is the cold snow outside the window, which depresses me further, but I feel more secure here than outside. I just came back from the warehouse area, the domain of my enemy—the warehouse lead. Even though he is supposed to report to me, the warehouse manager is nobody in front of a unionized person in this company. How can I feel like this? This is not normal. After all the real-life threatening situations as a firefighter and all the situations that involved gun violence in my home country, why can I not handle this amount of sabotage from the warehouse lead?

There is something wrong with me. I go through so many different emotions. One minute I'm laughing and having fun with my friends. The next, I'm crying because I'm afraid of what will happen to me at work.

The next day, it was decided I needed to do something to change this situation. But what situation? I do not know what is happening. First, I need to understand what is happening to me. I notice all these emotions resemble the conditions of my clients with depression. Let's take the evaluation to see what is happening. OMG! Forty-nine points out of fifty. I am seriously depressed. I need to consult other colleagues. I cannot handle this alone.

I am lucky to be part of Dalton Associates. *Let me talk with Dr. Dalton and find the best team of people to get out of this crazy depression.* It was not easy, but with an amazing team of people behind me, I decided to take some time off work to take care of myself and my family; one of the best decisions in my life, but the people at work did not think the same.

It is not comfortable to be sitting on the sick people's bench. I can feel how people look at me at the Mood Disorders Clinic at the University of Toronto. But the curiosity of seeing my brain on the qEEG brain map excited me very much.

After a couple of months, I was off medication, but I was not ready yet to go back to the office. I was feeling pressure from my friend that referred me to the company to get back soon because they needed me or they needed to hire another person for the position.

Against the recommendations from my therapist, I decided to get back to the office. Wrong decision. The news that I was on mental health leave was spread all over the company, and the judgment eyes were all on me. For two weeks, the pressure on me was worse than ever to the point that I was guided without noticing to present my resignation because "it was the best for both parties."

That was my last shot after ten winters of hard work in Canada. I will never be successful in this country. I need to go.

Thank God for the wife I have. She was my strength and my pillar during the slippery moments as an immigrant in Canada. And she understands it's not possible for me to continue fighting with a society that doesn't accept me as I am.

But I had a plan...

And as you will see before you finish this book, it was a good plan: a plan that allowed me to achieve happiness and well-being for myself and my family.

* * *

Do you want to be happy?

Do you want happiness for your loved ones?

Do you think everybody wants to be happy?

After thousands of years of looking for the holy grail of happiness, why do we find, over and over again, histories of people with anxiety, depression, stress, suicidal thoughts, etc.?

Will it be possible for you to eat the fruit of happiness at some point in your life?

And the certain response to that question is no. You cannot eat the fruit of happiness because happiness is not one fruit; it is more like a fruit salad.

When I shared with you my episode of depression in Canada, I only shared the miserable feelings created in my work environment. For sure, those job conditions were terrible for me—actually, not only for me. The person before me also resigned under severe personal depression (nobody told me that at the beginning). But certainly, that was not enough to put me against the ropes. I had much more than that on my hands. I was burning the candle at both ends for sure.

My wife and I were working different jobs. My son Samuel was a newborn, and Sabrina was two years old, and we did not have family support. I was worried about my parents' life back in Venezuela. The three properties we had at that moment needed my attention. It was much more than work-life unbalance. It was work-wife-kids-entrepreneurship-friends-finances-spiritual-immigration-physical health-emotional-weather-political-social-mental-career ... super unbalanced... you get the idea.

I did need to narrow the story to only my job-related problems in my first paragraph to get your attention. Our brains need to simplify all our problems to get a solution, and usually, the easy solution is to think that money will solve all our problems.

With time, humans have been noticing that money and power are not the only solutions or the only paths to achieving happiness. Work—our money/power center of life—was not the only important variable. Therefore the phrase "Work-Life Balance" was created with two groups to focus on, but guess what? There are many other groups in the happiness equation.

I do not think I need to expand much on the problem. People are suffering, and it is clear why. We all know that all or at least a big part of the happiness we see on social media is lies. All the beautiful pics and the fabulous reels do not project real people's happiness. The numbers show a different reality. Domestic violence, gun incidents on the streets, drug and alcohol abuse, suicidal cases, etc., are just the tip of the iceberg in a post-pandemic society where it is not clear if going back to the office is a good idea. Who will make the decisions? Who will be the less crazy political leader—"the one"—to handle this "new normal?"

We are living in unprecedented times in human history. Therefore you need to make unprecedented decisions to live the life you want, the life that you and your loved ones deserve.

In these moments, you cannot oversimplify the dynamic in a "work-life balance" relationship, but you also cannot overcomplicate it in a long list of to-dos to conquer the world as your favorite social media influencer is showing in their account.

So, where should you start? How can you organize all your dreams to achieve happiness in this book?

I will share with you a new human software called World Essence Bond (WEB), and with your help, I will install it in others to prepare us for the metaverse era.

The WEB will help you flourish and achieve the happiness you deserve.

Do you have it all figured out? Are you at the peak of your happiness?

Great. This book will help you maintain it, and you can pass it on to your future generations because life is hard, and things happen. You can prepare for any changes. This book will help you to be prepared for those moments without being over-worried about difficult moments.

Are you a work in progress? Do you have happy moments in your life but also extreme moments of sadness?

Don't worry. That's life. I am here at this point. Maybe you are here. Maybe sometimes you are here. Sometimes you have it all figured out. Life is like that—dynamic and changing all the time.

Maybe you can relate right now to my period of depression. Maybe you feel that a lot of people hate you. That your work sucks. That other people's lives are amazing, but you are stuck in a spiral of bad decisions and bad results. Do not worry. I have been there. There is a way to get out, and you can do it. The trick here is not to shoot for perfection—shoot for the next step.

"But Ignacio, what is the next step?"

To recognize the next step, first, you need to realize where you are right now.

Think about this. On this simple scale, -5 being hell on earth and +5 your perfect life, where are you located right now?

(-5)—(-4)—(-3)—(-2)—(-1)—(+1)—(+2)—(+3)—(+4)—(+5)

Throughout this book, we will move from minus five to plus five, from "I hate life" to "I have it all perfect." Well, clearly, you have free will. You can move in the other direction. But if you want to move in the other direction from +5 to -5, from a perfect life to "I hate life," this book is not for you. Close it now and go and be miserable.

If you want to be happy, successful, flourishing, and blessed, accept your talents, and bless others with your talents, this book will take you to the next level on this beautiful path that is worth walking, and we will walk it together.

During our walk on this book adventure, I will share with you five steps to change some basic things in your perception of happiness and well-being and rebuild them under your own standards.

I don't know if you like Frank Sinatra, but I really love the song "My Way." And I truly believe the only way to achieve happiness is to understand your own personal state of well-being. In this book, I will introduce you to five steps to achieving your own definition of happiness.

* * *

Maybe in the past, the expression "work-life balance" (WLB) was enough to achieve the American dream and achieve the desired happiness. But not now. I will show you in this book the reasons why you need to change this WLB paradigm to a new one. Around this new paradigm, we will build a new mental, emotional, and behavioral structure that will provide you with the tools you need to build your well-being path to happiness.

If you follow these five steps, you will reach your next level of fulfillment, and you will be able to stay there because you are building it with solid foundations.

But wait, there is more. You will reach a point where you will be ready for your next well-being level. And as you build your muscles in a gym after you learn how to use the machines, you will come back to this book and do it again; come back to these five steps and expand your happiness potential. The trick is to return to this book and do these five steps over and over again.

Everything in life is a cycle of practice. People believe that successful individuals are born with success because you only know that part of their life.

Dwayne "The Rock" Johnson is synonymous with the picture of what it is to be tough and stereotypically "macho." The Rock has a remarkable personal history, from his pro wrestling career to his present position as one of Hollywood's most incredible action movie stars. But he's realized, over time, that vulnerability is an omnipresent part of the human experience. In an interview with *People* magazine, the actor talked about how he struggled with mental health as a teenager. Since then, he grew the idea that there is nothing unmanly about reaching out to others when you require help.

The Rock put it this way; "The first time I had experienced depression, I was eighteen years old, and I had no idea what depression was," he said. "Back then, depression was also called 'get off the couch and get your shit together and change what's happening here.'

I was an only child, and I was always a better listener than I was a communicator in terms of sharing my feelings," he said. "And I feel like the most important thing, obviously, is communicating and realizing that asking for help when you're down and you're feeling wobbly or when you're depressed is actually the most powerful thing you can do. Asking for help is not a weakness. As a matter of fact, asking for help is our superpower, and men, especially us, we fall into this trap of being really adverse to vulnerability because we always want to be strong and feel like we can take on the world.

But the truth is you have to, and hopefully, over time, learn to embrace vulnerability and learn to embrace this idea that you can't always solve everything. A lot of times in life, as you head down the road, you're going to need help, and it's all a part of life."

In my own case, life has been amazing in general. I have lived a very prolific lifestyle. People believe that only billionaires can talk about a prolific life, but this is not true. I know happiness firsthand. I was born in Venezuela, and I lived there in the eighties and nineties before the economic and political crises of that beautiful country. I was a party animal and very successful with girls. Well, that was easy in a country that had ten beautiful girls per man at the parties. I visited every corner of my country, and I was successful in all my endeavors there.

But I not only know happiness firsthand, I also know depression very well. Not only because I graduated as a psychologist and worked with patients with depression. Not only because I lived on the streets of Paris, France, where 21 percent of the population suffers from clinical depression, or in Canada, where 20 percent of the population is depressed. It is because I suffered from it. And at that point in my life, it drove me to drastically change my direction in life and allow me and my family to achieve the well-being we are enjoying in our life right now. For this reason, I have dedicated time to this topic in my professional path, and I have learned from different perspectives the best ways and the best techniques to move from depression to happiness.

During my time as a psychotherapist, I had clients with different cases of anxiety and depression. During my work, I realized that the engineers were a little bit more successful with my program. It wasn't only that they stayed long after they achieved their initial goals. These types of clients stayed with me not only to improve their condition in relation to their depression, but they also wanted to change different things in their lives based on my working approach. I started creating different programs for my engineering clients based on the different goals they wanted to achieve.

For many reasons, at a point in my practice, I decided to learn about hypnosis, and the two areas by default to start working with hypnosis were weight loss hypnosis and smoking cessation programs—techniques that allowed me to bring more clients from the corporate world, my original area of work as an ergonomist. This opened a new window of opportunity and success for my techniques.

After they were successful in the initial goal, my clients wanted to use hypnosis in different areas of their lives. Therefore I started to design different programs for sports, career, and financial goals.

During this time, I also published my first book in Spanish focusing on organizational change, *Human Capital: A Manual for Change*, showing the way to apply ergonomic concepts to the changes companies had been experiencing in the previous couple of years.

After I wrote that book, I was looking to apply this knowledge to human resource departments, but they didn't pay much attention to it. On the other hand, individually, my clients were very interested in the concept of human potential in my proposal to find what I called the "ergon," their human function. In this process, I started working with different approaches that provided my clients with great success in different areas of their lives, and I noticed that they impacted different successes in different areas at the same time, promoting their general well-being based on the PERMA model presented by Dr. Martin Seligman, one of the many models you will use during your adventure with this book.

At the beginning of this chapter, I shared with you my situation with my depression and also shared with you the time that The Rock had his depression. These two examples, one very personal and the second very public, show you how two grown men (and The Rock is a very grown man!) were in a very fragile moment in their life.

And certainly, the goal of this book is not to heal clinical depression. It's important to understand that this book does not intend to be the solution to a psychological illness. If you need professional help, please seek support from a professional.

These examples are there to tell you that it is possible to come from the bottom of your human condition and start working on your progress to be better. This is possible. And while reading this book, you will discover and analyze your current condition—where you are right now.

I invite you to use tools to measure where you are in your initial state. I'm pretty sure you will be located in our scale line from -5 to +5 around a -2 or a +2. Around 70 percent of the population is on that measurement—in an area where not everything is amazing, but not everything is terrible.

Again, if you measure close to -4 or -3 and you feel that you need professional help, please seek that help, but for the majority of the people reading this book, that will not be the case. I'm pretty sure that you are a person that feels the need to achieve your full potential, and we're here to do that.

Reading this book, you will notice these changes in your life;

At +1: You will find personal moments of happiness. At this moment, you will work directly with yourself to achieve that personal happiness.

At +2: You will start feeling more synergy with others. You will start building more social support for your plans.

At +3: This is where weird things will start to happen—good but weird. New doors will open. You will find new opportunities. People that you need will show up, and you will start to see that fluidity is part of your life.

At +4: Magic will be a normal thing in your life. The law of attraction will be normal for you.

At +5: You will become magic. You will start creating miracles for others. You will be at a point in your life where you are able to help others because you are totally fulfilled in your own life.

The idea of this book is to maintain our life at levels between +3 and +5. Remember, life is difficult, and it is changing all the time. Therefore you will not be stationary in one fixed place, but this fluctuation can be maintained on the positive numbers. I am sure that you will prefer to fluctuate between +3 and +5 rather than -2 to +2.

Fluctuating between +3 and +5 will allow you to be happy, achieve the highest levels of well-being, and impact others to help them achieve their goal in life—to achieve their highest God-given potential.

Chapter 2 | Pay Attention to Your Life— Attention is the New Currency

Why do you work? Do you work for money or for a purpose?

"Knowledge has no value except that which can be gained from its application toward some worthy end." -Napoleon Hill

I could not believe it. He was so happy. I still remember my first movie in a theater. My dad took me to see *Popeye*.

I can still hear his laugh, "AAAHuuUUH GUhGuhGuhGuh." It is not possible. I still can't believe it. Robin Williams took his own life. He had all the knowledge to live a great life—you only need to see his movies or his interviews to see that. He was inspirational to many, not only with his jokes and acting but with his life-changing advice. And many followed his instructions.

What happened to this great man?

The truth is, toward the end of his life, Robin Williams was not able to use his own tools because he did not know who he was anymore. I truly believe his Lewy body dementia was a psychosomatic consequence of his decision to exchange health for money—a decision he took many years before his death.

I wish he had listened to his own advice.

"I said, 'Robin, why don't you go and do stand-up?'" she recalled. Robin broke down in tears. "He just cried and said, 'I can't, Cheri.'

I said, 'What do you mean, you can't?' He said, 'I don't know how anymore. I don't know how to be funny.'" —Dave Itzkoff, *Robin*

We need to know the importance of paying attention to our decisions on time.

People need to know who they are and how they serve others, focusing on the direction of their God-given potential. This great potential involves many areas in your life, not just one. It is not just about the way you make money. That's like putting all your eggs in one basket, and Robin did that for many years, being funny for money.

So, let's enter into the main problem, the Work-Life Balance. This amazing lie that tells you that you need to find "THE BALANCE" between how you make money (Work) and how you expend the money (Life). And in this perfect balance, you will find happiness.

For some generations, we were trained to go to school, achieve great things, and in that way, we would be accepted into a great university to achieve professional degrees, which would secure a great job for us. And that great job would provide us with the money to be happy.

But that beautiful tale was a big lie. A lie that many still believe.

Sure, money can help you to be free from some worries in your life, but it cannot make you happy. It is very interesting that for many years we thought the absence of suffering was equal to happiness, but the truth is that they are not the same continuum of variables, and I will explain this in depth in Chapter 8. For now, let's focus on this idea of working as a way to access money to be happy.

The pastor of my church, Potential Church, Pastor Troy Gramling, shared this article called "The Day America Told the Truth."

"And they surveyed some Americans; they asked these folks what they would be willing to do for ten million dollars. So think about that. What would you do for ten million dollars? If I said, 'I've got a check. It's ten million dollars, but you have to do something.' What are you willing to do for ten million dollars?

Here are the responses;

25% said they would abandon their family for ten million dollars.

23% said they would become a prostitute for a week.

16% said they would give up their American citizenship.

16% also said they would leave their spouse (some of you would do that for free, wouldn't you?)

10% said they would withhold testimony allowing a murderer to go free.

7% said they would kill a stranger.

3% said that they would put their children up for adoption.

Now those seem like drastic steps to me; I don't know about you. But ask yourself, why would anybody do those things?

It is because we really believe that ten million dollars would make our life better. That's the only reason that we would do something like that. Is the thought, the idea that if I could get ten million dollars, then: I wouldn't have to be stressed out about inflation, or I wouldn't have to worry about what is happening on the other side of the world, or I wouldn't .... (fill the blanks)

In other words, I could have a sense of peace and a sense that I got plenty of money in the bank."—Adapted from Pastor Troy Gramling preaching at Potential Church, Feb 22, 2022.

And I don't know if this idea of having plenty of money in the bank will give peace to you. I don't know if this is your paradigm, but in my house, I grew up with the idea that money was the only thing between me and my dreams. During my early years, my dad was like the "poor dad" in Robert Kiyosaki's book—a well-educated man with access to money but always suffering because it was not enough. I went to a private school where all the kids had the best of the best, and I was always limited. I was a poor kid at a rich school. I don't know if my dad was a millionaire with very cheap taste or if we had money problems, but that doesn't matter.

For many years, I operated in a "Bad-Money" paradigm that took me years of psychoanalysis to understand. For a long time, I thought that if you don't have it, you're anxious and worried all the time. But if you have it, you are also in a position of darkness, and you will be part of Dante's *Divine Comedy*. If you have money, you are on the path to meeting Lucifer, only gaining the pleasures of this world.

So there was a paradigm; there was a way that I looked at the world. And many of us see the world with the wrong paradigms or, at least, ones that separate us from our goals.

The paradigms related to money and productive life are, in general, or at least with the majority of my clients, in opposition to happiness and well-being.

And it was then that I started to notice the progress of my clients and the initial changes they made to achieve what they came to find in my office. I realized that the main barriers that separated them from happiness and well-being were concentrated on these five:

1. Their paradigm—profound beliefs about who they are and how the world functions—is opposite to their concept of happiness. ("I will be happy with money, but the love of money is the root of all evil.")

2. They do not have any other motivation, no purpose, aside from the motivation of reducing pain and increasing pleasure.
3. There is no real compromise to be happy or achieve well-being.
4. There is no plan to achieve happiness and well-being.
5. They ignore the first steps of the plan to achieve happiness and well-being.

And certainly, you can go through life with wrong paradigms and disregard this list that I just mentioned to you, and believe you are happy; but you are living a lie. Just look at Robin William's life or Jim Carrey, who is clearly a miserable person when he said, "I wish everyone could get rich and famous and everything they ever dreamed of so they can see that's not the answer."

I believe we experienced amazing lessons in the last couple of years (2020–2021). And I truly believe it is time you take control of your own life, your own happiness, and your own well-being. And make this change in your life, not only for your happiness but also for the future generations. I and you have the responsibility to share this knowledge. This is the purpose of this book.

The purpose of this book is that you find your ergon—your own path, your God-given purpose.

" . . . I played for the best college football team in the country, the University of Miami, the Hurricanes. We were national champions, and the number one goal was to play in the NFL, and that did not happen for me. That was hard. It was a hard kick in the gut. Because I'd worked for years and years and years to make it to the NFL, and I didn't. My friends around me were making it, and they were becoming millionaires and buying their parents houses. All the dreams that we all had, they were living the dreams that we had. And I was not. I was actually living a nightmare.

I fell into depression at that time, and what it took to get out of that was time and self-empathy. Being good to myself and recognizing that life goes on and this was not the path for me. As much as I wanted it to be the path, as much as I felt like I was doing everything I could to make sure that happened, it just didn't happen. It wasn't for me, and that wasn't the life or the path for me. And then I picked myself back up and put in the work with my own two hands and created another path." —Dwayne "The Rock" Johnson

Like The Rock, you can find your own successful path, and I will teach you how. In this book, I will mention some successful experiences with my clients in Canada, the US, and South America, but this book is not about them; this is about you. I want you to reflect on your own beliefs. I want you to reflect on your own paradigms: those inner enemies opposed to your success and happiness.

Maybe for a minute, you can close your eyes, take a deep breath, and look at your life. See how sometimes your own self, your deep belief, sabotages your progress toward the goal you want to achieve. Take a look at your life and ask yourself if you are always running from pain and looking for the pleasure that global marketing companies sell you. Ask yourself; Do I have to compromise to be happy?

I am very sure you have all the knowledge to be happy. I am here only to help you to organize your ideas. You have all the knowledge you need inside you, but for some reason, you always click the button "Do not upgrade."

Some companies force you to upgrade the software to slow down your cell phone or reduce the battery life. But here, I am talking about upgrading yourself with your own software, the one that was designed by your creator so you can achieve your God-given potential. Allow yourself to advance to the next level, overcome this ball and chain that slows you down, and whenever you feel stuck, return to the main barriers that separated you from happiness at any time and check if you are blocking yourself.

And please do not feel bad if you find this blockage in your life. You're not alone. If you research "work-life balance" on Google, you will find more than three billion searches for these words. Most people are looking for a golden work-life balance to find happiness and well-being. Many of my clients work in large corporations. In my past experience as a psychotherapist and I/O psychologist in Corporate America, I noticed how people were suffering, particularly in their psycho-social conditions. Now, especially after the COVID-19 pandemic, people are looking for meaning in their professions. They are looking for purpose within the companies, and a large portion of them have decided that meaning is more important than a job position.

The Great Resignation is a result of that. I have been insisting for many years that this would happen, but human resources departments have been blind to cries for help when the evidence has been right there in front of them. The Great Resignation has an impact on major corporations as well as the lives of those choosing to prioritize their passions.

I'm sure you are looking for this work-life balance in the same direction as many people do right now. In this world where remote work is more common, people are looking to enjoy their lives and work together, which we will be working on in this book.

If you follow the solutions this book offers you, you will be part of the group of people solving this situation. You're not alone in this problem. And the good news is that you will not be alone in finding the solution.

This book offers you a transition. And during this transition, it is very important that you have an open mind. It is essential to allow yourself to upgrade many things in your life.

One is the way that you perceive the world—the paradigm. The other is how you structure your habits. So we will be working on those and many others with different strategies throughout this book.

You need to value this change and must be open to it in your life. Remember the popular expression, "We cannot continue doing the same thing and expect different results." I know that change is not or, at least, was not common in our lives; and it's sometimes uncomfortable. However, you need to understand that we are living in a world that is changing very, very fast, and you need to be able to adapt and change quickly. So I will help you incorporate all these tools into your new life.

Even if they are tricky initially, you will notice that the habit will be part of your life after some time, and the magic will be natural in any aspect of your success.

"Learn the rules like a pro so you can break them like an artist."— Pablo Picasso

"Reality is negotiable. Outside of science and law, all rules can be bent or broken, and it doesn't require being unethical." —Tim Ferriss

You may be the same old, same old type of person. And you ask yourself if you need to do things differently. After all, this year, you have been doing it the same way, and you may think *maybe it's too late for me to find a different way of doing things*. And the response is NO; in these times, you need to be adaptable. You need to be able to see the rules differently. Maybe you think the only motivation is to reduce pain, take pills, and have a quick solution. Or increase the pleasure. *Let me just sign up for a cruise and enjoy the food and the alcohol without thinking about the consequences after returning from that cruise.* But there is a point in life where people need to take responsibility for what they do.

Maybe you don't feel like compromising either. And there's no compromising your body or your health.

But let me tell you something. If you don't invest in yourself right now, time will pass you the bill in the future. So it's essential to pay attention to your life and health.

Maybe you are a free thinker and, because of that, you don't like to compromise, but I'm not asking you to compromise with other people. Instead, I'm asking you to compromise yourself for your own happiness and well-being.

Maybe you'd like to live life one day at a time, and you don't want to plan too much of it. But you will see in this book that the balance between now and the future is essential; in fact, it's the only real balance that you need. You need to have goals to achieve in the future and enjoy the happiness of the now.

Let me assure you that this book can help you find all these solutions, especially to respond to all the questions previously in this chapter. You need to reflect on yourself because it's not all on us—"the experts." As experts in human development, psychology, or coaching, we are not here to give the responses. Actually, we are good at asking questions. So you need to self-reflect on your own process.

You can actually self-reflect on your definition of happiness right now. You can start responding to these questions, and at the end, you will see how your point of view related to these questions will evolve.

- What is your definition of happiness to this point?
- What are the most important things for you to be happy?

- What things are you pursuing right now?
- What else do you need to discover from your talents?
- What are your limitations to being happy?
- Are you happy being happy?
- Are you grateful for the things that you have right now?
- What else do you want to experience in your life?
- What is the successful formula for your life?
- Should you quit your job?
- Should you go back to school?
- Should you go on a diet?

We will be responding to these questions and much more during the book because you need to self-reflect on your own happiness. The tools in this book will give you the capacity to self-reflect and define your own happiness. That is the most crucial part of this book. You will need to ask many questions of your inner self.

* * *

But I had a plan...

In the first part of this book, my last couple of words were, "I had a plan." Yes, a plan.

After stopping my medication, I had a serious conversation with my wife. We needed to do things differently. So I told her we had two major choices. We could move out of Canada, or I could live my Johnny Depp lifestyle there, like Ricky Martin's song "Livin' La Vida Loca."

I was not able to handle the weird "social Canadian" restrictions on my behavior; simple regulations like you cannot use perfume, you cannot play loud music, you cannot talk with people and look them in the eyes, kiss them, hug them or touch their shoulder because they need their personal space, and you cannot discipline your kids because the state will take them away. Indeed, thanks to Jordan Peterson, I realized these rules were social-political indoctrination from the political left in Canada, but for me, at that moment, it was my only reality. That is a conversation for another book and something I frequently discuss when I'm a guest on podcasts.

The critical point here is that this personal separation from people, all this nonsense, political or not, literally made me crazy.

So I asked my wife, "Look, what do you want to do? We can go to Spain or to South Florida."

Before I continue, a short note. I know many of you reading this book are Canadians. Please don't get me wrong. I believe Canada is a fantastic place. But certainly, Toronto was not my city. The Golden Horseshoe was not for me. I have a lot of friends in Ottawa and other parts of Canada, and I love them. So, sure, it was possible to relocate to other cities. But my situation was too extreme at that moment. I just wanted to go to a different place. So we decided to move to Florida.

We planned ahead for two years. I decided to quit my job, sell all my properties, pause my psychotherapy practice, close down for business, and go back to school for a two-year social work program at Sheridan College.

The plan was to do those two years and the next day take an airplane and move to Florida. During those two years, we applied for jobs. We devoted ourselves to different strategies that accelerated the process, and we had the opportunity to move before those two years were up. Everything happened in a year, and during that year, I was able to redefine my life and work with different personal development programs. It was a fantastic year—a year that I went back to basics. Back to things that were natural for me when I was young—techniques like meditation, visualization, praying, and faith. I went back to my own self in a way that changed everything.

In that year, I noticed that I was able again to bring magic to my life, my relationship, and my family, and I decided that I would never quit it again. For a number of reasons, I had forgotten that magic. I lost it when I was tricked by the politicians in my country into getting into a political reality that was not mine. I lost my magic when I thought I was escaping from a terrible destiny in my country. I lost the magic when I got married and felt that as I was the head of the house, I needed to be responsible and work hard every day to provide the best things for my family, and I lost the magic when I thought that money was the main thing that I needed to produce to be happy.

During that last year in Canada, I realized that I was able to create magic in my life. Then when I moved to Florida, I arrived like a rock star. I published my first book, got interviews on radio and television, and received fantastic support from family and friends not only for my book and my presentations but also in my hypnosis business. Now I have a great training company called Ergon Academy. I recreated this magic in my life.

Everyone knows this magic—the moments when everything is fluid, working, and aligned. I can help you to get more moments like those in your life. Would you like that? We can do it together because I've discovered how, and I live it every day myself.

You can find this magic spot of fluidity. For sure, not everything is perfect; life is hard. But you will be in a place where you will take any punch from life as if you are made from solid rock. You will live in a place where life will not move you to depression or sickness. You will be able to receive those punches from life and get up because you will be in a good area. You will be in the positive spectrum of our model, the heart of this book. Being in that positive spectrum will bring you happiness and well-being.

And remember, this promise is not only for you, but you can also spread this knowledge to your partner, your family, and your friends, and you can create a better world for them: a better world for us all.

Chapter 3 | The Steps to Happiness and Well-Being

"But seek first the kingdom of God and His righteousness, and all these things will be added to you."—Matthew 6:33 (ESV)

Some of my clients are women with complex pasts with a history of sexual abuse when they were young, or in some cases, those sexual abuses were recreated by implanted fears against male figures. In any case, these memories and emotions are related to a sexual abuse structure that significantly affects their present relationship with their partners.

These clients usually request a regression process, to which I respond, "We could do that, but I'd like to do something that's actually much better."

In the words of Jason Linett;

"It's not so much that we are pulling out the magnifying glass and looking at the past and trying to understand what the problem was in the first place. It's more so, rather than a magnifying glass, perhaps a bit like a slingshot because our goal is actually to pull back with the intention of letting go. And now we are gonna use that momentum to propel you into the outcomes of where you wanna be. So you don't have to live back here in these patterns anymore, and it's all about where you are going."

So I will take you there, ready to build your life back. The above is a procedure that helps fantastically, but it needed something else.

I realized that my clients needed it to build their lives forward and, in this way, to be the best partner possible for others. Additionally, the best partner for them will show up.

If the person is at their best, if all these parts of the person are together, it will be easy for another person to show up in their life and be in love with them.

It is the magic solution; it is impressive how after my clients work on their character, on themselves, and gain their life for themselves, like magic, a new person shows up in their life. Finally, the perfect partner shows up. Nowadays, every time I see a client because they're having trouble finding their true love, I always say that the ideal partner will show up when they're ready. It's like this expression: "The master will appear when the disciple is ready."

Curiously, it is precisely the same formula for your happiness and well-being. They will show up when you are ready, and I will prepare you.

* * *

People always ask me in my presentations and training about coaching, "How do I know a coach is a good coach?"

A good coach always sets goals. Therefore, it is imperative to measure where you are and where you want to be.

I wouldn't be a great coach if I didn't follow my own rules, so let's set our baseline.

It's based on the positive psychology training that's one of our essential tools at my school Ergon Academy. We have a continuous -5 to +5:

| -5 to -4 | in the Clinical Psychology area | Professional support is required |

-3 to -2	struggling with life	Dependable
-1	struggling	Dependable
1 to 2	happy people	Independent
+3	biopsychosocial-spiritual well-being	Interdependent
+4	recreating your reality	Magic in your life
+5	one with the creation	Being the magic for others

This book promises to keep you fluctuating around +3. If you follow these instructions, you will never be lower than +2, and you will be able to access +4 at your peak. These states will allow you to maintain your happiness and well-being at high levels.

What about +5, you may ask? That state is known as the "Jesus state." Unfortunately, we do not have enough data to take you there or promise that this book will take you there. But I genuinely believe this book will give you a glimpse of how to live the good life, the one that will allow you to walk the path to the kingdom of God.

So, I have given you an idea of where we are going. The question is now where you are at. To measure the baseline of our well-being, we will use the PERMA profile tool at:

https://www.purposeplus.com/survey/perma-profiler/

Also, we will use an adaptation of the wheel of life designed for the areas in this book.

These two measurement scales are organized from 1 to 10, and we will translate them in this way:

-5 = 1	Clinical psychology
-4 = 2	Clinical psychology
-3 = 3	Dependable
-2 = 4	Dependable
-1 = 5	Dependable
1 = 6	Independent
2 = 7	Independent
3 = 8	Interdependent
4 = 9	Magic in your life
5 = 10	Being the magic for others

At the end of the book, there is an evaluation assessment. You should do it three times. I suggest producing two or more copies of it. The first time will be when you start the book. The second time will be after you finish reading the book; at that point, you will understand the concepts. Your evaluation may go down. Do not worry. You are on a development path. Sometimes we believe we are better than we actually are. After one month of writing down all your statistics and all the areas from this book, you should take the evaluation for the third time.

Do you want to be happy only at the end of this book? Or do you want to be happy all your life? This book will support you during the entirety of your life's journey.

It is like going to the gym. You will look good, but if you abandon the gym, you will lose your muscle capacity sometime after. So you will need to come back to this book from time to time in your life.

Excellent, you have your seat belt in position.

Are you ready for this ride?

Great.

We will enter the five steps—the core of this book— and you will see how all of this takes you to happiness and well-being. In Step 5, you will see how happiness is an essential variable of the positive psychology concept of PERMA.

Okay, here we go. Here are the five steps you need to take to be ready to receive great happiness and well-being in your life;

> Step One: Change the Old Paradigm of Work-Life Balance (WLB) For a New Paradigm; the World Essence Bond (WEB).
> Step Two: Meet the Four Levels of 'Emen.
> Step Three: Discover Your Essence.
> Step Four: Identify What the World Needs from You.
> Step Five: Bond Your Strategies.

Let's take a look at these key ideas in a little more depth;

Step 1: Change the Old Paradigm of Work-Life Balance (WLB) For a New Paradigm; the World Essence Bond (WEB)

In this step, you will review the WLB paradigm. You will learn that you need to find something that you love to do in your life and how to make it part of your life and not let anything separate it from you. You need to feel that you are playing, that you are enjoying life, and that you will achieve different things in this playing. Connecting with people, you will make good memories, and you will create money for yourself and your loved ones.

So that old paradigm of working separately from life, in different places, and bouncing from one side to the other no longer works for you or anyone else.

The WEB Paradigm

In this new era, in a world where we are living different realities, we have our personal reality, the political reality, the social media reality, etc. Now the metaverse is coming. We have various types of currencies—real currencies and cryptocurrencies. And we are starting to have real estate in the real world competing with real estate in the metaverse. What should we call it? "Fake Estate."

How can you have a great life living in this multiple-variable system?

Do not worry. In this book, we are preparing ourselves for this new WEB Revolution.

Step 2: Meet the Four Levels of 'Emen

Sometimes when I mention the word "ergon," people compare it with the Japanese ikigai concept or the dharma of the Buddhists. Actually, ergon is a natural term in our Western society, but we have forgotten it. Ergon was used by Greek philosophers and is presented more than 100 times in the Bible.

There's a reason why the ergon concept is more adaptable to our culture. Inside this way of observing the areas of our life, we will find four sections;

- What do we believe?
- What is our vision?
- What is our purpose?
- What is the plan?

Step 3: Discover Your Essence

You will look inside yourself to analyze the fourth level of the 'emen within each segment of your essence; your physical, mental, and emotional life and how these three participate in your character—a character that you enjoy in this life, the one you will present to your creator spiritually.

Step 4: Identify What the World Needs from You

First, we'll talk about your loved one. Then we'll talk about the legacy—kids, grandchildren, nephews, or your projects for the next generations. We will also talk about your social relationships and how others support your life. Finally, we'll talk about finances and your career.

Step 5: Bond Your Strategies

We will evaluate the strategies, and we'll connect them all together. You will find a way to bond all the strategies in each part of your essence and connect them with the strategies related to the world to establish this W.E.B. revolution.

Chapter 4 | Open Your Mind

Be ready for your new paradigm. Open your mind.

"Minds are like parachutes: they only function when open." — Thomas Robert Dewar

In his textbook *Principles: Life and Work*, Ray Dalio speaks about getting around the two most significant barriers to good decision-making—your ego and your blind spots. If you are like most people, you don't know how other people see things, and you are not good at trying to understand what they are thinking. In such a case, you are closed-minded; in such a case, you will close this book.

Still here? Maybe you are not closed-minded. Closed-minded people are too focused on telling others what they believe is right; they are more likely to make statements than ask questions. This is very important. You will notice in the middle of the book that my proposal is more about the fantastic technology of asking questions than telling you what to do.

This first step will not only help you to be happier and achieve well-being. Research suggests that open-minded people are cognitively complex individuals who are less swayed by singular events and are more resistant to suggestion and manipulation—very important for the marketing strategies we are encountering nowadays. Also, they are better able to predict how others will behave and are less prone to projection. And the one that I like the most because I have a 180 IQ—open-minded individuals tend to score better on tests of general cognitive ability such as the SAT or an IQ test. Sadly, it is not proven whether being open-minded makes one smarter or vice versa.

"They are coming. Please take all the documents you can, and save them." But what happened? They condemn him. They sentenced him to death. "Oh no, what are we going to do?" Can you guess who I am talking about?

For 1,600 years, Pelagius's name has been synonymous with heresy that attributed free will to man to exclude all divine influence on human decision-making. He has been seen as the embodiment of self-righteous arrogance by the traditional church. Yet there is no evidence that Pelagius taught that God played no part in human decisions.

He defended two ideas common in ascetic Christian literature at the time: that human nature was inclined to goodness and that man had free will.

He was against three intertwined doctrines that were being promulgated at the time by St. Augustine; original sin (everyone is born sinful, born with a built-in urge to do bad things), an absolutist account of prevenient grace (divine aid that directed the human will toward righteousness), and predestination interpreted as preordainment (taught predestination based upon God's foreknowledge).

Guess who won between Augustine and Pelagius? Well, there is a St. Augustine!

Paradigm, worldview, archetype: all these words are references to our way of looking at the world—the way we process the information we take from the world. Our Jewish/Christian culture impacted our ways of living and our way of thinking. Sadly, early Christians never understood that even the lives of many Jews were predestined by God for the sake of scripture fulfillment

(Augustine); Jesus came to remind us of our good nature and our capacity to choose—our free will (Pelagius).

What I am trying to explain here is that the parents of your parents and their parents before them were influenced by St. Augustine. Whether you are a Christian or not, if you live in the western world, anything in your life is seen through those glasses, including the way you see work in your life. It is clear that the concept of WLB is not something new. You can find it in the Torah arguments about the Sabbath.

Going back to our initial history, if you look at work through the lens of St. Augustine, work is a result of our sin—predestined for us—not to discover but assigned. If you look at work through the lens of Pelagius, work is an act of love from our good nature, and we are free to do it or not; we are capable of deciding if it is vital to rest on the Sabbath or not.

And I believe I have many paradigms in my life that I need to change—other people, not many. What about you? Do you have some ways of seeing the world that do not benefit you? And how will you decide which ones are the ones for you?

You will see that my proposal here is straightforward and will help you define your worldview without losing your connection with others.

The point of this first step is that you open your mind and allow some changes in your worldview. And I know it is not easy to identify your paradigms and change them. I understand some models work for some people but not for others. Maybe you like Augustine's proposal or Pelagius's or a mix between them. Maybe you have your own model of seeing your life, but you do not share it. Maybe you are afraid to share it. You do not want to be burned at the stake or crucified—not literally, of course—but it may happen to you on your social media account.

Throughout this book, you will find new ways of living that will work for you because this whole plan will be designed by you for you; therefore, do not be afraid to accept your own new paradigm.

This new paradigm will be built around the acronym WEB. World, Essence, Bond. Yes, within this book, you are Bond... World Essence Bond. With a license to kill... the old version of you, lol! Like James Bond. Forget it, it's a bad joke.

We will deconstruct and reconstruct five critical areas of your essence as a person and five critical areas of your relationship with the world, and we will bond them with interlinks to form your life plan.

Essence Areas:

1. Physical health (Strength)
2. Intellect (Mind)
3. Emotions (Heart)
4. Character
5. Spiritual self (Soul)

World Areas:

1. Love
2. Legacy
3. Social
4. Finances
5. Career

At the end of this book, we will bond them together to give you the most simple plan to achieve your happiness and well-being.

I believe we have encrusted on our very deep archetypes an unbalance that is much more important than the WLB. It focuses on the areas of the Essence and the areas of the World.

Just imagine that Augustine's team is focused on service to others for this argument. You are a sinner, and the only way to find happiness and salvation is to gain it through God's grace, and you earned the grace by doing good actions for others. We are trying to see our value and success in the world areas somehow. If you know the concept of work-life balance, work includes finances and career, and life has love, legacy, and social living, but something is missing; the most crucial part is missing—"you."

On the other hand, on the Pelagius team, it is the contrary; you are not a sinner. You are perfect, created in God's image, and you became a sinner in your relationship with others, specifically in the wrong relationship with others. But, as an individual, you are perfect and free to choose as Adam in Paradise. You are free to choose your own essence.

Before Martin Seligman bet all his casino chips on positive psychology, he studied the phenomenon of "learned helplessness" and "learned optimism." His research was initially on the learning process, but nowadays, it's used for different psychological phenomena like depression or theories of happiness.

It would be great to sit down with you and have a coffee at Starbucks (where I am right now writing this book) and connect all the little dots between Augustine and learned helplessness and Pelagius and learned optimism. But I would like to ask you for a little leap of faith, and I will appeal to the concept of presupposition. That being said, I will not go deep into many of the arguments; I will just present some ideas as they are authentic. Maybe you think otherwise, or your family and friends think otherwise, but I will ask you to play along with my thoughts and see if they take you to the promise of happiness and well-being that you are looking for.

Seriously, I ask this not only because it will save me money on ink and paper or because fewer pages will make this book more affordable in the end. It is about the placebo effect, the Jesus effect;

your faith will save you. Your trust in this book will motivate you to finish it and apply all the ideas I'm bringing to the table. It will allow you to connect your essence with Pelagius, who I think is the real father of personal empowerment. Do not worry. My proposal is simple; I am tapping into biblical wisdom and many centuries of deep philosophy, but with the tools of positive psychology, the journey to achieving the happiness and well-being you deserve is a piece of cake.

The essential presupposition of this book is:

Seek first the Essence and his righteousness, and all the World things will be added to you.

During all the years of Dr. Stephen Covey's working with successful individuals, he discovered that high achievers were often plagued with a sense of emptiness. I did not understand this in 1997 on my first reading of his book *The 7 Habits of Highly Effective People*, but nowadays, I can give the same testimony after many years of professional practice. To understand why, Dr. Covey did deep research, and he noticed a historical contrast between the two types of success.

Before the First World War, success was attributed to ethics of character—characteristics such as humility, fidelity, integrity, courage, and justice. After the war, success was attributed to personality, public image, behaviors, and skills. As a result, there was a shift in what Covey refers to as the Personality Ethic—creating a phenomenon of quick successes that overlook the more profound principles of life. Covey argues that your character needs to be cultivated to achieve sustainable success, not your personality.

I believe this dance between Personality Ethic (World) and Essence is much older than the First World War, and we will see it again and again in human history. And success in the long run—particularly happiness and well-being—will go to those who focus on their essence.

Chapter 5 | Faith: Presuppositions, Vision Purpose, & Strategy

"If you can believe," said Jesus, "everything is possible for one who believes ('emen)."—Mark 9:23 (NIV)

It's a beautiful day. The sun is shining, and the sky is blue. I always enjoy playing in the pool, splashing in the water, and running around with my friends. In this state, I feel happy and content. But suddenly, something changes. I felt a coldness in my heart, a sadness that I had never experienced before. I look over and see my little brother floating lifelessly in the pool. Without thinking, I ran to him and pulled him out of the water. I screamed, "Help, Dad, Dad," but it was too late.

I can't believe what is happening. My dad jumps into the pool and takes him away from my arms. Everything turns to chaos; people cry, and my mom is praying out loud. Some doctors sitting around the pool come to help my dad and my brother, who is only two years old. He is not breathing.

One of the doctors takes his tiny body and hits him against a chair so he can spill out all the water and the food that he had previously consumed. They try and try to help him breathe, but nothing is happening. One of the doctors insists on taking him to the hospital.

They run to the car, and I run after them. But they are running fast; all of them go and leave me behind.

I take my bicycle, and I put all my energy into following that car, but they go too fast. I see them getting further and further away. I am getting exhausted, so I stop there in the middle of the street, confused and sad, with just one question in my mind. What will happen to my brother?

But before I finish the story and go deep into the concept of this chapter, I would like to ask you. How do you want to be remembered when you die? This is a question that often haunts people, and for a good reason. It's essential to think about our legacy and what we want to leave behind.

Most people do not take the time to analyze their lives. They go through the motions, living day by day without a plan or purpose. This is a recipe for disaster. To achieve success in life, you need to assess four crucial parts in the essential areas of your life; the parts I call the Four Levels of 'Emen: The presuppositions, your vision, your purpose (why), and your strategy to implement.

And how does this connect with my brother's story? Well, the rest of the story is a story of faith.

They did a couple of procedures to help him at the town hospital. But nothing worked. My uncle Marcos, my brother's godfather, was able to send a military chopper to pick up my brother and move him to the capital, Caracas.

After a couple of hours in the hospital, in the waiting room, as the doctor walked out of the room, my parents knew that their son was gone. Indeed the doctor came out to tell my parents that my brother was dead.

After a couple of minutes that felt like an eternity, a nurse came out of the room screaming, "Doctor, Doctor. The kid. He's alive." So they went back to the room to work on him for a couple of hours. Finally, almost twelve hours after the event started, my brother was stable.

Every time I tell this story, people ask me, "And he was all right?" To which I respond, as a big brother must, "I think he had brain damage. He is a little stupid, you know." Lol! I am just kidding; brothers joke. He graduated as an engineer, and he is brilliant. Well, sometimes!

This event marked our life. He was declared clinically dead around thirty minutes. This was a miracle from God. My mom prayed to God from the moment we realized he drowned in the pool, and we thought that there was a miracle, a resurrection. I was only eight years old, and this was a very moving moment for me.

From that moment on, there was no doubt in my faith. Since I was born, I have been a Catholic church member. I was hit by a car and passed over my body when I was five, and I survived, and my brother's resurrection was clear proof that God exists; if you ask me if I have faith in God, I will say, "Of course."

Actually, I do not really understand the question anymore. Faith in Jesus is natural for me. But how can I explain that if people do not understand the meaning of the word faith? They do not have faith in themselves, others, or God. Therefore, it is essential to know what faith means before asking you to have faith in yourself and practice your faith.

This book is not meant to prove that I have exceptional theological comprehension; instead, it is my attempt to shed light on certain aspects which should assist you in rethinking your life and future. As a result of this statement, I'd like to make some Bible comments.

Again I want to mention Mark 9:23 (NIV), "If you can believe," said Jesus, "everything is possible for one who believes ('emen)." I took this to imply that when Jesus said, "who believes," he was not using the Greek word "pisteuo" since he was speaking in Aramaic. The Aramaic Bible records that he used the term 'emen, which is comparable to the Hebrew word 'aman translated as "rock of support, assurance, be faithful." Some people connect it with the word amen, which we use today.

The critical part here is that 'emen is pisteuo (faith) and ergon (work), wrapped in one word.

There is no appropriate word in Greek or English to render the word 'emen. You can only describe 'emen. That is why James says that "faith without works is dead." (James 2:26 NIV). He is saying pisteuo without ergon is dead.

Great. We have two parts of 'emen. But also I found the word pisteuo (faith) can be decomposed into two parts; Believe, in philosophy, "propositional faith/faith-in," and Visualize, in philosophy, "non-propositional faith/faith-that."

"Now faith is the assurance of things hoped for" (visualize), "and the evidence of things not seen" (believe).—Hebrews 11:1 (AMP)

On the other hand, the Bible uses the word "ergon" in many ways. Two of the meanings are very common. One is our motivation, or why we do what we do (human function). The other is an action or a series of actions that we do on purpose (deed).

"For the Son of man is as a man taking a far journey, who left his house and gave authority to his servants and to every man his ergon (work) (why, purpose), and commanded the porter to watch."—Mark 13:34 (KJB)

"And Moses was learned in all the wisdom of the Egyptians and was mighty in words and ergon" (deeds).— Acts 7:22 (KJV)

I can confidently say that you can accomplish anything you want in life if you have faith: Presuppositions, Vision, Purpose, and Strategy (Deeds).

Presuppositions:

Presuppositions are assumptions that we make about the world around us. We all have presuppositions that we hold on to, whether we realize it or not. For example, we might believe that all people are basically good or that the universe is ultimately fair. These beliefs shape how we see the world and how we interact with others.

Presuppositions can also be dangerous; if we base our decisions on flawed presuppositions, we may make poor choices. That's why it's essential to be aware of our own presuppositions and to question them from time to time. Only by doing so can we ensure that our beliefs are accurate and that our decisions are sound. Neuro-linguistic programming (NLP) and hypnosis are fantastic practices to design your own presuppositions.

Vision:

Your vision for life is what YOU want to achieve. It is YOUR dreams and goals. Nobody else can tell you what your vision should be—only YOU can decide that! Once you have clarity on your vision, you need to develop a strategy to make it a reality. This is where many people fall short. They have all the motivation in the world, but they don't know how to take action and make their vision a reality. I would recommend to you to see the documentary *The Secret*; it will give you a good understanding of the concept of vision.

Purpose (Why):

Your purpose is WHY you are doing what you are doing. It is your reason for getting up each day and taking action toward your goals. Without a vital purpose, it is effortless to give up when things get tough. But if you have a clear purpose that inspires you, then you will be much more likely to stick with it and achieve success. The book *Start with Why* by Simon Sinek can provide you with good information about this point.

Strategy:

Finally, your strategy is your plan of action. It is how you will execute your vision and achieve your goals. Without a robust and well-thought-out strategy, your life will likely flounder. To create an effective strategy, you'll need to think about your goals, how you'll achieve them, and what resources you'll need. A sound strategy will help you focus your efforts and ensure that you make the best use of your time and resources. In Chapter 9, "Bonding Strategies," I will use an adaptation of *The 7 Habits of Highly Effective People* by Stephen R. Covey to support you with your strategy.

Up to this point, this book has given you powerful technology that you can use in any part of your life. We usually think of technology as a computer, but technology is the use of science to create new things, improve human life, or change the world. You can use technology in anything; you can use it to buy groceries or to send a rocket into space. This reflection on the word "faith" will help you understand many things about your life and what you want to achieve in the future. Do it as a simple exercise; do you have faith that you will succeed in the supermarket doing your groceries today? Simple. What are your presuppositions, vision, purpose, and strategy for that endeavor?

If you want to achieve success in any area of your life, it's essential to take a step back and assess the four crucial areas we've discussed. The presuppositions set the stage for everything else that follows; your vision provides focus and inspiration, your purpose gives meaning to what you do, and your strategy is how you will put all of this into action. Once you have a clear understanding of these essential elements, don't hesitate to use this fantastic technology to help you attain the success you desire. Let's follow along on this fascinating journey into the world of happiness and well-being!

Chapter 6 | The Components of Your Essence

"In the unlikely event of an emergency landing and evacuation . . . oxygen masks will drop down from above your seat. Place the mask over your mouth and nose like this . . . if you are traveling with children, make sure that your own mask is on first before helping your children."

Have you thought about why the flying attendant gives you this critical instruction?

"If you are traveling with children, make sure that your own mask is on first before helping your children."

For me, it is clear that no matter who you are, you cannot help others if you do not help yourself first. This is true in all areas of life, from personal relationships to work and career success.

Therefore you need to focus on your personal happiness and well-being before you impact others. When it comes to your personal health and happiness, you need to focus on these five key areas: physical, mental, emotional, character, and spiritual. By paying attention to all five of these areas, you can ensure that you are living a happy and healthy life.

Developing these areas is personal work; therefore, it is essential to define a personal presupposition, vision, purpose, and strategy for each area. In this chapter, I will provide some examples in each area, but you must ultimately come to your own conclusions. It is up to you to find meaning in life and create your own identity.

There is no one-size-fits-all approach to achieving success or happiness. What works for one person may not work for another. Each individual must find their own path in life and follow it regardless of what others think or say. Let's start with the examples;

* * *

1. Physical:

Taking care of your physical health is essential for overall well-being. Defining physical health can be a complex task as there are many different factors that contribute to a person's overall well-being. Traditionally physical health was defined as the absence of disease or severe illness. However, with the advent of modern medicine, life expectancy has increased dramatically, and as a result, our definition of physical health has evolved. Today physical health can include everything from the absence of disease to fitness level.

There are many different components that make up physical health, but some key areas that should be addressed include physical activity, nutrition, diet, reducing alcohol and drugs, medical preventive self-care, and rest and sleep. By making healthy choices in these areas, we can help to improve our overall physical health. However, it is essential to remember that physical health is not just about the absence of disease; it is also about feeling good and having the energy and strength to live life to the fullest.

Physical Presuppositions

It is important to note that there are certain general presuppositions of health that must be met for an individual to be considered super healthy. You have your own; please take what works for you; if some do not work for you, disregard them or create the ones you need;

a) The individual must have a basic fitness level. This means that the individual must be able to perform the activities of daily living without any undue fatigue or stress.

b) The individual must have a balanced diet. This means that the individual must consume various foods from all food groups to obtain the nutrients necessary for good health.

c) The individual must have a sufficient amount of rest and sleep. This means that the individual must get enough sleep each night and should not feel excessively tired during the day.

d) The individual must have a positive attitude toward his or her own health. This means that the individual must believe that it is possible to improve their health and well-being through lifestyle changes and positive thinking.

Meeting some of these presuppositions of physical health is great but remember, you have your own definition of physical health.

Physical Vision

To achieve your fitness goals, you need to be able to see them in your mind. This means feeling it with your own senses and being able to create a draft, writing a vision statement for yourself, a vision board, a mind map, etc. This statement should answer the following questions: What is your ultimate goal? What does this look like? Once you have a clear picture in your head, it will be easier to work toward it, for example: "I am physically healthy and fit. I eat a balanced diet and get enough sleep each night. I exercise regularly and enjoy being active. I have the energy and strength to live life to the fullest."

Physical Purpose

What is the purpose of the human body? The purpose of the human body is to facilitate the body's energy pathway (energy input, energy storage, work output, and heat release) in order to maintain the conditions necessary for life and allow you to accomplish those things which are essential to you. The purpose of the human body is to keep you alive and to allow you to do the things that make you happy. When your body is healthy and functioning well, you are able to live a happy and fulfilling life. When your body is not functioning well, you may experience pain, illness, and disease. It is essential to take care of your body and to make sure that it is functioning at its best in order to live a purposeful life.

Find little purposes for little tasks first. "I want stronger arms to bring the groceries home" or "I want to walk my dog in the morning and at night. It will bring me health, and I love my dog." Do not shoot for big ones at first, such as "I want to run a full marathon tomorrow." All purposes need to be cyclical in relationship with the strategy. Every success after applying your strategy will give you more "purpose energy," or what I like to call "emotional salary."

Physical Strategy

A strategy is a plan of action designed to achieve a major or overall aim in any area of life, usually used in business or big projects, but we can use it in specific areas of our life. The human body is no different; in order to get the body you want, you need to have a purpose and a plan. The purpose of this section is to provide you with an example of the strategy of the human body and how you can get the body you want. You should know what body you want at this point. You have the presupposition, the vision, and the purpose of the body you want.

The human body is an amazing machine that is able to adapt and change according to our needs and wants. However, in order to get the most out of our bodies, we need to have a clear purpose and plan. Without a purpose and plan (ergon), our bodies will simply follow the path of least resistance, and we will not achieve our desired results. So what is the strategy of the human body? In simple terms, the strategy of the human body is to be happy and healthy. When we are happy and healthy, our bodies are able to function at their best, and we are able to achieve our goals. And how do we achieve happiness and health? There are many ways to achieve happiness and health, but one of the most important things you can do is to focus on your wellness. Wellness is an all-encompassing term that includes physical, mental, emotional, social, love, etc.

"Hey Ignacio, I see what you are doing here in this last paragraph. You are already bonding all the areas of the wellness concept."

Great, you are so smart, but do not get ahead too fast. We will talk about the B (Bond) of WEB in a couple of chapters. Let's go back to your body strategy.

There are many things you can do to promote health and wellness in your life. Eat healthy foods, exercise regularly, get enough sleep, and avoid harmful substances.

By taking care of your body, you can _____

Remember, it is your strategy. For me, it is; by taking care of my body, I can live a long and purposeful life.

* * *

2. Mental:

Mental health is often neglected, but it may be more essential than physical well-being. I do not say this because I am a psychologist;

53

we all know the saying, "The mind is its own place and in itself can make a heaven of hell or a hell of heaven." That is because your mind is in command of your life; if you do not consider the actions you are taking, you can die. We see it every day and wonder what the person was thinking.

Mental health includes our emotional, psychological, and social well-being. It affects how we think, feel, and act. It also helps determine how we handle stress, relate to others, and make choices. Like physical health, mental health is essential at every stage of life.

There are many different factors that can contribute to good mental health. Some key areas include positive self-esteem, resilience, optimism, and effective coping.

Mental Presuppositions

When you are thinking about what beliefs you want to have in this area, remember that your beliefs will influence your thoughts and actions from now on. So make sure they are empowering beliefs that will help you. This is really important!

Maybe you are inexperienced in this area, but you can start by believing that your mind is the greatest asset on which you can rely. Your ability to think well is everything. As a result, you can start respecting your intellect. How intelligently you live your life is the best indicator of real intellect. And one of the most important things in this book is that you can choose to think, and you can choose what to think about. Remember, I'm only giving you examples here. You need to write down your own mental presuppositions.

Here it's essential to stretch your idea of what your brain is capable of. The majority of people consider intellect to be the most important function of their brain, yet your brain has numerous other capabilities, including memory, equilibrium, processing math and science problems, reading comprehension, and so on. Don't restrict your mind's potential.

Mental Vision

Previously I asked you to not limit your presuppositions about your mental capacity. Here, in your vision, I'm asking you to go wild. I never believed that my brain was capable of comprehending English, and yes, you read that (in English) correctly!

There are numerous mountains to climb, especially intellectually. Do not allow your own intellect to limit your vision.

For me, my vision in this area is clear. I need to keep learning new things so that I can improve my life. I want to think positive, empowering thoughts all the time. I will not let negative or limiting thoughts get in the way.

What is your vision for your intellectual life in the long run? How do you see yourself fitting into this area in the future? What can you do to raise the bar in this area?

Mental Purpose

Please take your time here and find your own purpose, your "why" for your mental purpose.

On the B (bond), I will ask you to come back and review each in relation to the others, and you will see that many of the areas depend on this one, therefore your mental purpose will affect the other areas and vice versa. For example, the refusal to consider using your brain may destroy a career if you don't allow yourself to perceive how things are changing and commit to learning what you need to know in order for your work to not be outdated. If you make the decision to think, pay attention, and learn, your chances of success will always improve. Refusing to think, pay attention, and learn can ruin a marriage. If you don't listen to your spouse and keep doing the same things over and over again, it will cause problems in your marriage.

Mental Strategy

A strategy is a plan of action designed to achieve a specific goal. In business, strategy is often thought of as a long-term plan, typically spanning several years, that sets out an organization's overall goals and objectives. "Yes, Ignacio, you already mentioned the concept of strategy before." That is true. But I did not point out that the word "strategy" in this book is more similar to the Agile methodology than extensive project management.

The Agile methodology is a type of strategy used mainly in the tech industry. It breaks the project into several phases—in our case, levels of 'emen on Essence and World (WE). And it always involves collaboration with stakeholders, for this book "Bond" (B). In Agile, teams cycle through a process of planning ('emen at WE), executing (bonding), and evaluating during the project.

The human mind is an incredibly powerful tool, but it's not always used to its full potential. To get the mental health you want and be mentally sharp, you need to repeat and stretch. Your brain will get better and better if you repeat and stretch. A significant difference between my first book and this one is that in my first one, I overwhelmed people with information; in this one, I repeat and stretch. If you feel that I am saying the same thing over and over again, that is okay. I am deepening the knowledge with repetitions, but do not rest all your attention on this. Pay attention to your reading because, at any moment, your brain will stretch.

* * *

3. Emotional:

Emotions are the mental and physical states that we experience in response to events in our lives. It's like the whole body is the brain. They are typically classified as positive, negative, or neutral. Emotions can be mild or strong, and they can last for a short time or a long time.

We deal with our emotions in different ways. Some of us like to express our emotions openly, while others prefer to keep them bottled up. Some of us are good at managing our emotions, while others find emotions difficult to understand and control. Whatever our approach to emotions, they play an important role in our lives.

Our emotions are how we feel but also affect how we think and how we behave. They can impact our physical health and well-being. When we're happy and optimistic, we're more likely to take care of ourselves and make healthy choices. When we're sad and anxious, we're more likely to neglect our health and well-being. Our emotions can also affect our relationships with other people. When we're happy and content, we're more likely to be kind and caring toward others. When we're angry and resentful, we're more likely to be unkind and rude. Emotions are a powerful force in our lives, shaping who we are and how we live.

It is important to manage your emotions in a healthy way. Recognizing and dealing with your feelings can help you reduce stress and live a happier life.

Emotional Presuppositions

Whatever your presupposition in this area is, it is very important to understand that all emotions are necessary. Do not reject any emotion. Understand that any emotion is a signal from your body that needs your attention.

Your emotions are a deep source of wisdom about yourself. They are signals from inside you that tell you something about the world around you. Emotions usually tell us to do something. For example, that uneasy feeling in your gut might be your body's way of telling you to be careful. It is very important for you to understand your emotions. The more you try to resist an emotion, push it down or ignore it, the louder that emotion will tend to become.

In my case, emotions are very important. I am a very passionate person, and everything in my life is full of emotions. For that reason, I have a very close relationship with my emotions. I allow them to go wild sometimes, like a golden retriever in a park without a leash. I allow them to flow. I cry like a baby. I fight, I love, etc. But I do my best to give them the proper space to do it. Therefore you will not see me at a funeral talking with people. I will be praying and crying. I will not be seated at a party. I will dance all night long. I do not go to a class if I am not going to give 100 percent of my attention. I am all in with my emotions, but using emotional intelligence, I canalize all the emotions to provide power to my WEB.

Emotional Vision

It is clear that the media, in all its genres, is manipulating your emotional states, especially your vision of what emotional state you should have. I received a call from one of the TV stations that used me as a psychologist for their shows.

"Segovia, how are you doing?"

"I'm great—super happy."

"How can you be happy? You don't know anything about the shooting in Texas?"

"No, what happened?"

"Hey Segovia, where do you live? Under a rock?"

It's not that I'm not sensitive to these life events. On the contrary, I am very sensitive, so sensitive that I need to isolate myself from events I do not have any type of control over. Every time I go to a radio or TV station, the vision of my emotions changes totally. It is impressive how I lose control of my emotions. I get anxious, worried, and sad; nobody notices it, but when I come back to my house, my wife notices the change. And it is totally normal. My body is reacting to the attacks of external situations. You should notice it too. If you don't, stop any contact with external information in your day-to-day life, and you will see the difference. "But Ignacio, you cannot live isolated." Why not? Isolated from what? I am well informed about what I need to know.

Pay attention to your emotional vision. I believe it is the area where we receive more attacks, and we do not notice. Build it and treat it like a little baby you need to protect.

Emotional Purpose

Although we often think of emotions as something that gets in the way of rational thought, they actually serve a very important purpose. Emotions are our brain's way of processing information and helping us to make decisions. When we feel an emotion, it is because our brain has determined that this is a relevant piece of information that we need to take into account. For example, if we feel happy when we see a friend, it means that our brain has processed the information that this person is important to us and that we want to spend time with them. Similarly, if we feel fear when we see a dangerous situation, it means that our brain is trying to protect us from harm. In other words, our emotions are actually a form of guidance that helps us to navigate the world in a way that is safe and healthy for us. Without emotions, we would be lost, and with too many strong emotions, we would also be lost.

Just take some time to find the things you need emotions for, why they are there, and the right amount of emotions required for that purpose. Play in your brain the Shave-a-Balloon Challenge. To win that, you need to find the proper amount of energy to shave the balloon without exploding it. Many things in your life need the proper amount of passion, happiness, and excitement, etc.

Emotional Strategy

Everything that we are doing here in this book is to establish this great strategy that will make you happy, that will establish your well-being and your success. At this point, you can see a pattern already. There are things in your life that make you happy. The more you repeat those things, the happier you will be. It is that simple. From smiling to jumping from an airplane, all of that will trigger a number of chemicals in your body that will shoot your emotions. Play with them, be the master of your life, be the master of your emotions.

I have been practicing meditation, mindfulness, and hypnosis for a couple of years already. You just need to do it. It is like going to the gym. It is like cleaning your teeth or making your bed. It is about just doing it. Schedule dinners with your loved one or best friends once a month and visit the comedy club, the art gallery, and the theater. You cannot use money or time as an excuse. And sure, sometimes your life is not at the point to expend all the money and time on things that you enjoy, but you can plan, and you will achieve it.

Before I moved to Canada, I was working as a highly paid consultant in Venezuela for engineering companies, but in Canada, I could only get a job as a pharmacy cashier. During that time, all my peers at the pharmacy were miserable about their lives and their work; but I went every day on time to the pharmacy with a big smile—happy about my freedom, my security, and the pharmacy discounts. One day one of them asked me, "Why are you so happy all the time?"

I said, "I am happy because this is just a step toward my bright future."

People do not see that they need to fall forward. If you fall forward, even if you fail, you will advance in your life. Here is your opportunity to go forward with your emotional strategy.

* * *

4. Character:

Your personality is made up of your personal characteristics. It's what makes you who you are, and it includes everything that matters about you. Your actions, thoughts, ideas, motives, intuitions, judgments, temperament, preferences, and tendencies all influence how you perceive yourself.

Character is what enables you to be happy and healthy and to achieve well-being. It's the foundation upon which your life is built, and it's the source of your strength and resiliency. When you're working on developing character, you're working on becoming the best possible version of yourself. You're striving to become someone who is honest and trustworthy, someone who is kind and compassionate, someone who is clearheaded and sensible. You're working to develop strengths and abilities that will serve you well in all aspects of life. Character is the key to a good life. It's what enables you to create lasting relationships, find fulfillment in work, and contribute to the world in a meaningful way. Character is the cornerstone of happiness, health, and well-being. So if you want to create a good life for yourself, start by working on your character. Become the best person you can be. You can start right now.

Character Presuppositions

Character is what allows us to withstand the trials and tribulations of existence. It is the ability to maintain our sense of self in the face of whatever life throws our way. Hardships come for all of us, but it is our character that allows us to face them with purpose and determination. Achievement comes through character. It is our character that drives us to put forth the extra effort required to reach our goals. Success, both in life and business, requires character. It is our character that allows us to maintain our sense of well-being in spite of everything. Character is literally a survival strategy. Without it, we would not be able to cope with the challenges of life. Character is what makes us human.

I had the chance to meet, talk to, and get to know police, military, and marine personnel. It's amazing how a good character is actually a life-saving quality. It might determine whether you live or die. Self-discipline is one example. Being unruly and irresponsible in a war zone can result in your death.

Now you can write some solid phrases as pillars for your character. This will be your compass in your life.

I can share with you my pillars in one phrase:

"I am Ignacio Segovia, the Ergon from the Phoenix Order." This is my character.

The fiery one on your path to success. I help people to find their purpose and strategy to serve only the resurrected, the Phoenix— Jesus Christ.

Character Vision

A good character is someone who has a clear vision of what they want to achieve in life and is willing to work hard to achieve it. They have a positive outlook on life and are always looking for ways to improve their well-being and the well-being of those around them. They are confident in their abilities and know that they can overcome any obstacle that stands in their way. They possess the courage to take risks and always give 100 percent effort. They are honest and always strive to act with integrity. They are compassionate and care about the needs of others. They are responsible and always put the interests of others before their own. They possess the determination to never give up and always strive for success. A good character is someone who possesses all these qualities and more.

Whether you realize it or not, your character is the most important aspect of your life. It is what defines you as a person and determines your level of success. If you want to achieve greatness in life, it is essential that you consciously choose your character traits. Look at the people you admire most in life and try to emulate their character. By doing this, you will be well on your way to achieving your dreams.

Perhaps the gap between who you look up to and your own character exists now. There's a lot of potential for your vision if you picture yourself closing this gap.

Character Purpose

I'm going to start with a well-known statement at this point. Every area in your life project has a strong gravitational pull on the others. Simply said, everything in your life is influenced by your character. You want a fantastic love connection? You'll need personality qualities like empathy, compassion, and goodwill. What's it going to take for you to live a healthy and active lifestyle? It will require personal qualities such as self-control, dedication, and responsibility. You'll need to have characteristics such as honesty, integrity, and dependability in order to make more money.

Character Strategy

Any leader worth their salt is going to tell you that character is the key ingredient to becoming extraordinary. But what exactly do they mean? Character is the inner quality that gives you the strength to face your fears and keep going even when things are tough. It's what allows you to pick yourself up after a setback and dust yourself off. People like Winston Churchill, Gandhi, and Nelson Mandela became extraordinary by summoning courage in the face of fear. They became extraordinary by persevering until they were exhausted, and it seemed impossible to even take another step forward. By coming up with a solid plan that would carry them forward even if they got pummeled, they became remarkable. Why? Because character is built in the face of adversity and your responses to that adversity. It's not built-in comfort or ease. It's a built-in challenge and struggle. And that's where you find out who you really are. So if you want to become extraordinary, don't be scared of adversity. Accept it and create a strategy to confront it. You have the power to shape and make yourself the person you were meant to be.

* * *

5. Spiritual:

At this point, it is clear to you that I am a Christian, and here I will not give you a Jewish/Christian lecture. Even though I am strong in all my life categories, it is not my intention to influence your definitions in any area of your life. I am simply sharing my concepts with you—concepts that were passed down to me by my predecessors but which are considerably more sophisticated and distinct from my parents' or grandparents' beliefs. I made a great effort to transition from religion to a personal and spiritual connection with God.

And that is my proposal in this section. Take the time to find a profound relationship with your creator. Where do you come from? Why are you here? Where are you going afterward?

Spiritual Presuppositions

In this section, I propose that we take the time to find a profound relationship with our creator. Spirituality entails the experience of oneness. One of the most important things that spirituality addresses are the deep questions of life that we all face at some point: Who am I? What is the purpose of life? And what happens when I die? When we ask ourselves these profound questions and seek answers from a higher power, we often find a great sense of peace and calm.

There are many ways to connect with our creator, but one is the experience of being benevolently connected to all that exists. The spiritual world offers a different perspective that can be very helpful in finding our way through life's difficulties. It is a source of support, strength, and guidance. Spiritual principles can help us live more moral lives and make wiser choices. They can also help us resolve personal conflicts and deal with difficult life situations.

However, before we can benefit from spirituality, we need to understand its presuppositions. We need to realize that spirituality is not a religion or a set of beliefs. It is an approach to life that encompasses all aspects of our being—body, mind, and spirit. When we live spiritually, we seek to connect with our higher selves and with the divine source of all life. We strive to become more altruistic, loving, and compassionate beings. We develop character traits such as patience, kindness, forgiveness, and humility. We work to become more selfless and less egocentric. In short, we strive to become better people.

Spiritual living is not easy. It requires commitment, effort, and practice. But the rewards are well worth the effort. When we live spiritually, we find a deeper sense of meaning and purpose in life. We experience greater joy, love, and inner peace. We become more compassionate and loving people, and we make a positive difference in the world.

Spiritual Vision

A spiritual vision can be defined as an understanding of reality that is based on intuition rather than on empirical observation. This type of vision is often described as a "higher" form of awareness, and it is typically associated with a deep sense of peace and well-being. For me, spiritual vision is the foundation of my spiritual path. It is what motivates me to seek out new experiences and to grow in my understanding of myself and the world around me. My spiritual vision gives me a sense of direction and purpose, and it provides the fuel for my personal journey of self-discovery. Although my spiritual path may take many different forms, it always starts with the quest for a deeper understanding of reality. And that quest begins with developing a clearer vision of who I am and what I am here to do.

My spiritual vision is constantly evolving, and it has taken many different forms over the years. For example, when I was younger, my spiritual vision was focused on finding a way to connect with God. As I grew older, my focus shifted to understanding the nature of reality and the role that I play in it—my ergon. Today my spiritual vision is centered on living in accordance with my highest values and principles. No matter what form it takes, my spiritual vision always leads me back to the same place: a deep sense of peace, love, and contentment.

Spiritual Purpose

Mark Twain was onto something when he said that the two most important days of your life are the day you're born and the day you find out why.

Discovering your true purpose may provide significance to your life on a whole new level because it has some significant answers. What is the purpose of your life? What is the meaning of it all? What is your objective in life? Why are you here?

Some people think that everyone has a purpose which they receive from the day they are born. The belief might be obvious to all, or it may be hidden deep within. In everyone, however, it manifests itself and has a function.

When it comes to finding out the meaning of your life, some people believe that it's something you're supposed to figure out on your own. The main objective is to be happy and at peace with yourself. A sense of contentment comes from within, not from what surrounds you.

Have you ever wanted to know more about yourself? Do you want to be in control of your life and how you live it? Finding this out is a really gratifying and satisfying experience. It can help you to make sense of your life and give it direction and focus. It can provide a sense of satisfaction and meaning that nothing else can quite match. So how do you go about finding your purpose? The first step is to tune in to your intuition. This is the part of you that knows things beyond the reach of your conscious mind. It's the voice of your higher self, and it will never steer you wrong.

There are many ways to connect with your intuition, but the simplest is to quiet your mind and listen to your heart. Pay attention to the things that make you feel good. These are the things that are in alignment with your purpose. Follow your bliss, and the universe will open doors for you where there were only walls.

Your intuition will never steer you wrong, so following it is a surefire way to start uncovering your purpose.

Spiritual Strategy

"By their fruit, you will recognize them. Do people pick grapes from thornbushes or figs from thistles?"—Matthew 7:16 (NIV)

Spiritual growth is not a spectator sport. It's something that we have to actively participate in if we want to make any progress. Just saying that we want to be more spiritual isn't enough. We have to have a strategy and plan for how we're going to make that happen. And ultimately, it comes down to our actions. What are we willing to do on a daily basis to become more spiritual beings? Are we willing to meditate, pray, or read religious texts? Are we willing to be more compassionate and loving toward others? If we're not taking action steps toward our goal, then it's all just talk. Actions speak louder than words. So if we want to live up to our potential as spiritual beings, we need to start taking action. Otherwise, it's all just lip service.

The first step to spiritual growth is acknowledging that we need to grow. Just like we need to eat healthy food and exercise to maintain our physical health, we need to put effort into growing spiritually. It's not going to happen automatically. We have to be intentional about it.

I can help you at the moment you are ready to go deeper. I use many tools to support my clients in this process and to respond to all these questions. Hypnosis, meditation, positive psychology, and mindfulness are some of them. A thorough and deep process on this might take you two or three months to complete, but do not worry about that. Today just start with basic steps. So find a notebook and start working on each step. When you finish, you will have a better understanding of your happiness and well-being and how to change it for the better.

If you're feeling overwhelmed by this chapter, don't worry! You don't have to learn everything at once. Just take it one step at a time. The most important thing is that you get started.

Chapter 7 | Invest in Relationships That Make You Happy

It's late, and I'm on the floor, waiting for my sleep time on a thin mattress. Time passes. I'm gazing at the shadows produced by the curtains on the wall, and I'm concocting stories with them.

I'm smiling because I just acquired a brother, and I'm incredibly pleased; I'm thinking about all the games we'll play together. Suddenly, for no apparent reason, I have a fantastic notion: why only one brother when I can have more?

"Mom, I'd like another brother, please. When will the next baby be born?"

"This is the last one, I assure you," my mother says.

I feel sadness in my heart and the running of tears I cannot control. I am weeping, but not for much. My father got tired of it. "Ignacio, why are you crying?"

"I want an abundance of aunts and uncles for my children, and it's impossible if I have only one brother."

Maybe you do not understand but let me put it in context. On my dad's side, there were seven siblings and twelve on my mom's side. So I had many aunts and uncles and an army of cousins. Being around many people was "the good life" for me.

Your relationships are the most crucial determinant of your happiness. The people you spend your time will directly affect how you feel emotionally and physically. If you surround yourself with positive, supportive relationships, you're more likely to be happy and healthy. But if you have consistently negative relationships, that's where you're going to experience the most pain, negativity, and stress.

It's essential to invest in relationships that make you happy and support your well-being. Spend time with loved ones, close friends, and people who make you laugh. These social connections are crucial for a happy and fulfilling life.

The relationships with people around you can be defined by the type of relationship you have with them. Usually, it's classified into three types: family, friends, and acquaintances. Family is a relationship you are born into, friends are people you choose to be around, and acquaintances are just people you know.

The social relationships problem can be found in places where people interact. And when there are more animals on the farm, there's more shit to clean. Some examples of places where the problem of social relationships can be found are home, schools, workplaces, and social events. These problems can make it difficult for people to get along and cause stress.

Many people will say there is no one-size-fits-all solution to the problem of social relationships. But I know that you can create one for yourself, and we will work together to do it. In the first part of this chapter, I will give you some examples of how you can solve some problems in your relationships right now. Then in the middle of the chapter, I will invite you to organize them based on your social priorities. Therefore at the end of this chapter, you will have your own solutions.

Let's talk about what you can do to be a better leader in your most important social relationships. Remember, they can sound simple to you, but I will stretch your mind at a point. So read these basic recommendations first. Even if they look straightforward to you, I repeat common or simple ones. In the four levels of 'emen, you will stretch your mind.

Excellent. Let's begin with some general examples of your social relationships.

If you have kids, you can be more understanding and patient. Kids are learning and growing, and they are going to make mistakes. As a parent, it is essential to be there for your kids and help them learn from their mistakes.

If you have friends, you can try to be more supportive and understanding. Friends sometimes go through tough times, and they need someone to help them get through them. So it is essential to be there for your friends and help them get through the tough times as a friend.

Lastly, if you have acquaintances, you can try to be more social and friendly. Sometimes people feel uncomfortable around others, but if you try to be sociable and warm, it can make them feel more comfortable around you.

Being a better leader in your most important social relationships can make those relationships stronger and happier. Let me list some ideas for our brains here:

- Social relationships are those with people around you.
- Social relationships can be defined by the type of relationship you have with them.
- There are three types of social relationships: family, friends, and acquaintances.
- Family is a relationship that you are born into (we will focus on love and kids).
- Friends are people that you choose to be around.

- Acquaintances are people you know but don't have a close relationship with.
- The social relationships problem can be found in any place where people interact with each other.

A common and simple problem in my office; Alice was having a hard time at school. She was always getting into fights with her classmates. Her parents didn't know what to do to help her. They had tried talking to her, but she just wouldn't listen. One day, they decided to take her to see me.

First, I helped Alice learn how to better deal with her anger. I showed Alice how to express her feelings more constructively. I also taught her how to communicate with her classmates better. And that provided her with some tools that improved her situation. But the most important part was that we worked on her presuppositions, vision, purpose, and strategy related to her personal areas—Essence—and the Bond of those with her presuppositions, vision, purpose, and strategy related to her friends.

As a result of the WEB approach, Alice's social relationships improved to the next level, and we will talk about that in this chapter. Alice was able to make friends and get along with her classmates. She even became a leader in her class.

Alice's story shows that social relationships can be improved with the help of the WEB strategy. Any Sunday magazine can give you tips if you have trouble with your social relationships, but the WEB strategy will take you to the next level. You may be surprised at how much it can help!

Ask yourself. *Do I have trouble with social relationships? Do I feel frustrated because I don't know how to connect with people?* Well, don't worry, you're not alone. Thousands of people face the same issue every day. However, there are some things that you can do to be a better leader in your social relationships.

The first step is to be aware of the problem. Once you are aware of the problem, you can start to look for solutions.

One solution is to communicate with the people around you. Talk to your family, friends, and acquaintances and let them know what's happening. This will help them understand your situation, and maybe they can offer some solutions of their own.

Another solution is to set boundaries. If there are things that you don't want to do or that bother you, let the people around you know. This will help them understand what is acceptable and what is not. It will also help keep the relationship healthy and strong.

Remember that building solid social relationships takes time and effort. Don't give up if things don't go right the first time. Keep trying, and eventually, you will find success.

Social relationships can be challenging to navigate, especially when there are problems in how we communicate with each other.

One of the best ways to become a better leader in social relationships is to learn more about ourselves and how we communicate with others. By understanding our own communication style, we can learn how to adapt our communication style to better match the communication style of the person we are interacting with. This can help to improve our relationships with the people around us.

Another way to become a better leader in social relationships is to focus on our most important relationships. For example, if our family is important to us, we can work on strengthening those relationships by spending more time with our family, talking to them more often, and listening to what they have to say. We can also work on being better listeners to our friends and acquaintances, which can help us build stronger relationships with them. By focusing on the most important relationships, we can become better leaders in social relationships and improve our social interactions.

When I was younger, I struggled with social relationships. I don't know if "struggled" is the proper word. For example, a group of guys once came to my university to assault me physically. Two of them were supposed to be my friends. At first, they did not know it was me, but they did not help me after noticing. One of them shook his head and said in a loud voice, "Tu si te metes en peos." It translates roughly into, "You are a troublemaker."

I had ADHD, and I thought a little differently, which got me in trouble. For example, at nine years old, I got bitten and kicked on the floor by more than seven kids from my classroom. I was mentally, emotionally, and physically abused all my young life by my peers and my oldest cousins, and although I had access to my dad's gun, I never thought of shooting any of them. Well, this is a conversation for a different book.

I'am trying to show you here that I was never good with people. But nowadays, you would look at me without noticing that. I had a long walk to achieve the level of social relationships I have today. It was not easy, but it taught me many things to share with my clients.

My clients often come to me with social confidence problems. I help them by teaching them the same techniques that I learned. As a result, many of my clients have seen great success and now have happy, fulfilling social lives.

If you're struggling with social confidence, there are things that you can do to improve your situation. One thing you can do is seek out social situations and practice being around people. This will help you become more comfortable with social interaction and allow you to practice your social skills. Another thing you can do is to work on building your self-confidence. This can be done through positive self-talk, affirmations, and visualization. Once you have built up your self-confidence, you will find it easier to interact with others.

All these recommendations can help you to solve a problem. But remember, you are not here only to solve a problem (-5 to -1). You will take it to the next level (+2 to +4). Take control of your social life.

We have already mentioned possible solutions. Now it is time to build them on the three more critical areas of your social relationships; love, legacy, and friends—the three first areas of the W in WEB.

When we think about relationships, the first thing that typically comes to mind is a romantic partnership. But relationships can be so much more than that. We have relationships with our parents and siblings, grandparents and cousins, bosses and coworkers, friends and neighbors. These relationships are essential in different ways, and they all require us to relate to others.

The term "relation" comes from the Latin word meaning "to carry back or bring together." When we relate to others, we bring them into our lives and connect with them on some level. Whether we provide support or comfort, share laughter or tears, all good relationships should yield something positive for both people involved. Good relationships make us feel we are part of something larger than ourselves and help us feel connected to others. They provide us with a sense of belonging and can even help to improve our mental and physical health! So the next time you're feeling lonely or disconnected, reach out to someone you care about and strengthen your relationships. You may be surprised at how good it feels.

As we journey through our WEB, we will encounter many different types of relationships. In the WEB model, these relationships are categorized as either romantic love relationships, parent-child relationships, or social relationships. Every kind of relationship offers its own unique set of challenges and rewards.

For example, in a romantic love relationship, we must often learn to compromise and communicate effectively to maintain a healthy relationship.

Parent-child relationships can be challenging because children are constantly growing and changing. As parents, we must learn to adjust our parenting style to meet the needs of our children.

Social relationships can be both rewarding and challenging. We may have disagreements with our friends and family members, but these relationships also provide support and companionship.

Ultimately, it's essential to remember that all relationships require effort and patience to thrive.

Welcome to the first three parts of W—love, legacy, and friends.

* * *

Love

No matter what your current love relationship status is, it's helpful to think about what you want your ideal love life to look like. This exploration can help you understand what steps you need to take to move closer to your ideal. We will start by thinking through every aspect of your ideal love life so that you can get a clear sense of what it would entail. This exercise can be beneficial regardless of your current relationship status, as it can help you identify areas in which you would like to see improvements. Whether you are in a great relationship that you would like to make even better or starting from scratch, thinking through your ideal love life can help you create a road map for getting there.

Love Presuppositions

People have various ideas about love relationships. Some people feel that females can't be trusted, no matter how lovely they appear at first. "They'll turn on you eventually." Others think that men always lie, deceive, and abandon their partners. "All women are only interested in his money" or "All men are simply interested in having sex with her."

These are just a few examples of people's many beliefs about love. But what lies beneath these beliefs? What are the presuppositions that give rise to these views? In other words, what are the assumptions people are making about love relationships?

One possibility is that these beliefs arise from a lack of trust. People may not trust that the person they're involved with will be faithful or honest with them. They may not trust that the relationship will last or that it will be fulfilling and satisfying.

Another possibility is that these beliefs arise from a fear of intimacy. People may be afraid to get too close to someone else for fear of being hurt or rejected. They may be fearful of being vulnerable and exposing their feelings to someone else.

Whatever the underlying reasons, these beliefs about love can negatively impact your final goal. As in the other categories of your essence, you need to find the presuppositions to support your overall plan. Presuppositions about love are assumptions people make about love relationships. Presuppositions about love can apply in any relationship, whether romantic, friendly, or familial. In this area, we are focused on your romantic one.

Why do presuppositions about love matter?

People who have presuppositions about love sometimes form these beliefs based on other people's experiences. These beliefs can be harmful in relationships, leading to mistrust and fear even before you have your own experience. In addition, these beliefs can color our view of all relationships and can make it challenging to form close connections with others.

When it comes to presuppositions about love, time is often a factor. People may believe that relationships always go through certain stages and have a set timetable for how things should progress. They may believe that once a certain amount of time has passed, for this or for that reason, the relationship is doomed.

These beliefs can be harmful as they can exert pressure on relationships and cause people to feel like they're not doing things "right." It can also lead to anxiety and frustration as people try to conform to these expectations.

You must think about your own presuppositions, write them down, and evaluate them.

Love Vision

A vision of love is a mental image of what love should be like. It can be based on our own personal experiences or on what we've seen in movies, TV shows, or read in books. Remember that you have control over your own vision. You may use the pictures of others to construct your own, which is your design.

The concept of a vision of love matters because it can help us create the type of relationship we want to have, regardless of our past experiences. If we have a clear vision of what love should be like, we are more likely to make choices that will help us achieve that vision and lead us to that love. Having a vision of love can also allow us to stay positive and hopeful in difficult times.

The idea of a vision of love is for anyone who wants to have a better relationship.

When you love someone, you have positive feelings toward them. You also care about their well-being and often put their needs above your own. Love is often described as a feeling of strong affection and requires both positive and negative aspects, such as patience and sacrifice. To love someone, you must first understand them. Even if it is a visualization, see yourself being your best for another person and that person receiving what you have to offer.

Do not ask the genie in the bottle to bring you the best partner possible. Instead, visualize yourself being the best partner possible and see how another person will react to the love you are bringing to the table.

Love Purpose

Love is a powerful and universal emotion that brings people together. It is the driving force behind many relationships and can be a source of comfort and strength. While love has many purposes, it ultimately brings happiness to those who experience it and those around them.

Why does love matter? Love is essential for human happiness and well-being. It forms the foundation of solid relationships, families, and friendships. When love is shared between two people, it creates a bond that can never be broken. Love is what makes the world go round!

It's the love in a relationship that determines who you become. Your love for each other made you as much as the relationship did. The love in a partnership is to blame for who you become.

The goal is to build a fantastic love relationship that will radiate so much positive love and good energy toward each other for years to come.

You may discover something new when you're no longer one-dimensional individuals who haven't grown as a couple. That's the goal of this category: love isn't only about two people gazing into each other's eyes all the time. Instead, it's about two people holding hands, facing life together in the same direction, and looking outward side by side.

Love Strategy

Love is one of the most critical aspects of our lives. A strategy for love is a plan of action that will help us attain our vision of love. It might include being more patient and understanding with our partners or being more spontaneous and adventurous to create a passionate love affair. By having a strategy for love, we're taking the necessary steps to make our vision of love a reality.

This strategy for love is for anyone who wants to have a better love life. Whether you're in a relationship and want it to be more stable and comfortable, or you're single and looking for a passionate love affair, this personal strategy will help. By having a plan for love, we're taking the necessary steps to make sure that we get what we want out of life.

One way to bring our vision of love into reality is to think about what we need to do daily to make it happen. For example, if we want to have a stable, comfortable relationship with a partner, we need to be more patient and understanding. On the other hand, if we're going to have a passionate love affair, we might need to be more spontaneous and adventurous. By thinking about how our vision of love can become a reality, we're one step closer to making it happen.

* * *

Legacy

I like to call this area legacy because it is about the next generations. It can be your children, stepchildren, nephews, etc. In my case, they are my kids; therefore, I will dedicate this section to being a parent.

Parenting is not easy but is the most beautiful and rewarding experience. It's an intellectual, emotional, and spiritual journey that just can't be duplicated in any other way. Being a parent or even just being around children and being involved in their lives can be one of the most rewarding things.

You may see your child's face light up with delight when they see you approach. You reach for their hand and take it, and your heart sings with love. As a parent, you undoubtedly know how much pure pleasure, joy, and laughter children can bring. Yet, on the other hand, parenthood has been described as one of the most challenging occupations in the world.

But we do it because we love our children unconditionally and would do anything for them. So if you are thinking about becoming a parent or are already one, remember that you are doing something unique. You are shaping the future, and the world will be a better place because of the children you are raising today.

Legacy Presuppositions

The presuppositions of parenting are the solid railway's rails, which will guide a trip to an unknown destination. Parenting is an ongoing process that is never really finished. There are no guarantees that it will be easy, but it is always worth it.

Pay the necessary attention here because it matters. It is the foundation of the parenting journey. It reminds us that parenting is an ongoing process with no guarantees of an easy outcome. The parenting journey is filled with both ups and downs. There are times when it's easy and fun, and there are times when it's challenging and frustrating. The critical thing to remember is that parenting is a journey, not a destination. Set your presuppositions to enjoy the ride!

Legacy Vision

Most parents, however, don't bring much of a mindfulness approach to bear throughout the process. But it's different for us because we have a tool that wasn't available before. The WEB will assist you in gaining clarity on your personal, parental, and child relationships. That is simply a huge benefit.

How would you want to act as a parent? As a role model? What kind of relationship do you want to have with your children? How do you see their lives unfolding over the coming years while in your care? What kind of a family do you want to raise? These are the questions you will want to look at as you create your vision for this category.

Parenting is not just about raising children to be independent and capable adults. It's also about creating a legacy that will continue long after you are gone. So what kind of parenting style do you want to be remembered for? What kind of values do you want to pass down to your children? These are all critical questions to consider as you begin parenting.

Parenting style applies at every stage of a child's life, from the prenatal stage to when they reach adulthood. Your vision for parenting should be based on what you want for your children, not on what you think other parents are doing. Every child is unique, so it's essential to tailor your parenting style to fit their individual needs. Stay mindful of your goals as a parent and make sure that your actions reflect those goals.

Vision in parenting matters because it's one of the most important aspects of raising a child. A parenting vision provides direction and purpose for parents and gives children a sense of security and stability. Children need to feel that they are part of something larger than themselves, and a parenting vision provides that sense of continuity and connection. Parents who have a clear vision of their parenting style are more likely to successfully raise happy, healthy children.

Legacy Purpose

The purpose of parenting matters because it is the foundation upon which children build their lives. It shapes their views and helps them understand why they do the things they do. Everything starts with parenting, and it must be done in a way that upholds the values of the family. This sets an excellent example for children and helps to ensure that they grow up to be responsible and contributing members of society.

Parenting is not just about raising children but also about passing on values and virtues to them so that they can continue the cycle of good after we are gone. This concept applies everywhere, but parenting takes on a special meaning when it is done in a way that upholds the values of the family.

The most essential factor is that we want to raise exceptional children who will have extraordinary lives because we love them and desire the finest for them.

Legacy Strategy

To make your parenting vision a reality, you first need to create a plan of action. Break down your parenting vision into specific goals that you can work toward. Make a schedule and set deadlines for yourself, and track your progress along the way. As I already mentioned, parenting is a journey—not a destination—so be prepared to make changes as needed. Stay flexible and always keep your child's best interests at heart.

And it's not just about handing down values to our children and hoping for the best. We have to be role models ourselves. We have to live the values we want our children to learn. That means doing more than just saying the right things. It means putting our money where our mouth is and walking the talk. It means being honest, kind, patient, and generous—everything we want our children to be when they grow up. And if we do all that, if we raise our children with love and purpose, we can know that we've done everything to give them a good foundation for a bright future.

* * *

Friends

Humans are social beings. We all have this deep desire to connect, communicate, exchange ideas intellectually and emotionally, and have discussions. Those with whom we have a fundamental connection are considered friends. They share our likes, opinions, and feelings and provide us with support. Friends make life more enjoyable, and they can be a great source of comfort during difficult times. Friends can also be a great resource, providing helpful advice and support when we need it. Good friends are worth their weight in gold, and we should cherish them.

We want human companionship on this trip through life. We won't be able to survive without it. It's not absolutely necessary for our survival, but we live more happily and fully when our social demands are met. According to studies, we perform better and live longer.

Friends Presuppositions

There are many different presuppositions about friends depending on your social culture, but friendships generally require time, energy, and investment to be successful. They don't just happen on their own. Friends also need to be unique to justify the investment.

Presuppositions about friends matter because they dictate how we interact with others. Friendships are a two-way street, so it's crucial to have the correct presuppositions to maintain healthy and beneficial relationships. Friendships are also a great way to build trust and rapport with others.

Take a few moments to state your presuppositions in this highly crucial area of life right now.

Friends Vision

Most people see friends as people they can rely on, talk to, and spend time with. They want friends that they can trust and be themselves around. Friends are essential for socializing and networking, and many people view them as an extension of their family.

The vision of friends applies in all aspects of life. Friends provide support and can be an excellent resource for information and advice. They can also help you have a good time and make memories.

Friends matter because they can help us achieve our goals and dreams. The vision of friends can be different for everyone. Some people may want to go out and socialize as much as possible, while others may prefer smaller gatherings or one-on-one interactions. Friends can also provide different things to each person; some people might need advice, others might need a listening ear, and others might just need someone to have fun with. The important thing is that you figure out what you want and then take action to make it happen. Friends don't just fall into your lap—you have to put in some effort to make them a part of your life.

Friends Purpose

Friends provide a sense of connection and belonging and a support system that is beneficial to both physical and mental health. Friends help us define who we are and where we fit in the world— giving our lives purpose. Friends also encourage healthy behaviors such as exercise and socializing, which have their own benefits for overall health.

There is a significant correlation between the quality of your personal relationships and your health, happiness, and financial success. Our relationships—our marriage, family life, and social existence—are the key to a happy, successful life. So there's an enormous purpose there, isn't there?

Nailing this category is very important. It will help you in many ways throughout your life. You can rely on it for support, energy, and guidance. That's a hugely powerful "Why."

Why are you striving for something that has to do with developing a fantastic connection with your family members and having great quality friendships? These relationships will require time and effort. They'll need money, care, and perhaps even some luck. So why is it worth it for you to do that? What will you obtain from it? Take a minute to think about the end goal of your social life vision.

Friends Strategy

Friends are essential, and we should have a strategy for them. Friends are there to help us in good and bad times, and we should be there for them as well. Friends can help us achieve our goals, but we need to put a plan in place to make sure that happens. Friends can also help put us on track and make sure we stay on it, or sometimes it's the opposite, so pay attention.

Like most people, I didn't think much about this area when I was younger. I didn't know what kind of social life I wanted. I had no particular vision for this space. When it came to my social goals, I had no filter; worst of all, I lacked a sense of who belonged in my life and who did not.

But after being forced to relocate from my country, I realized I was utterly alone. At first, all I wanted was some pals; any pals would do. So when I initially moved to Canada, I was overjoyed. As a kid, I'd always dreamed of living in that great nation, and now my ambition had come true. However, as the years passed by, I grew increasingly lonely. My family and friends back home were missed.

At that time, I regularly threw parties at my home to socialize with new people. I advertised the event to all my neighbors and waited for the night of the party to arrive. But it was always the same, one party after another: no real friends. Yes, people came over to my house, and we had a fantastic time. However, as the night progressed, more people left my party until only one person remained: my wife. I was always so disappointed! I'd been looking forward to making some new pals at my get-together, but it appeared that wasn't going to happen.

I eventually discovered that I'd have to plan something if I wanted to make friends. I needed to find methods for meeting new individuals who were pursuing the same things in life as me.

Nowadays, in this sector, my life is moving on a new path; I'm not where I want to be, and perhaps it's one of my weakest areas. However, since establishing a strategy in 2019, I've seen significant improvement. Even though the conditions of 2020 caused everyone to be socially injured, my social relationships improved in quality.

* * *

"Someone told him, 'Your mother and brothers are standing outside, wanting to see you.' He replied, 'My mother and brothers are those who hear God's word and put it into practice.'"—Luke 8:20–21 (NIV)

That was Jesus's goal, his essence, his primary aim. God's word and its application. What is your essence, your WEB? Are you brave enough to quote Jesus' words to others around you? My friends are those who know and support my WEB.

I discovered that I didn't need any more siblings after finishing my WEB. Even though I adore my brother and family, they have little involvement in my WEB. And that's just fine because now I understand it. I would love to go back and tell my six-year-old version, the one that cried for more siblings, that it's okay. The crucial people your kids will need will be there for them.

In the same way, your love, your kids, and your friends will be there for you if you design these three essential areas of your WEB. So pay attention to the four levels of the 'emen. Find your faith in each of these areas, and you will enjoy a life full of happiness and wellness.

I love the smell of this Spanish restaurant. The decor is so lovely, and the appetizers are amazing. My wife is talking with the birthday boy on my right side, and on my left side is an empty chair. A woman in her early forties arrives and asks me if she can sit on my left. She has a nice body and a lovely face, but she is not attractive. We introduce ourselves, but my wife is so loud in her conversation that we do not have more opportunities to exchange ideas. We get into the table conversation. As always, the comment pops into the conversation in the middle of the night, "So Ignacio, you do hypnosis." Usually, it's followed with "Can you hypnotize me to make more money?" or "Can you hypnotize my wife to clean the kitchen?" or even "I'm sure you hypnotized your wife to come out with you!"

I quickly respond, "Yes, of course." I always do it. I hypnotize her, and she hypnotizes me with love. "Aaahh, so lovely," the lady says.

It was a nice party, but the interesting thing was that the lady on my left did not participate much during the night. She approached me at the end of the night and asked me, "Do you have a business card with you? I believe I need your help. I'm obsessed with my ex. Can you help me with that?"

"Sure I can."

I didn't hear anything from Maria (let's call her Maria) until finally, after six months, she called me and said, "Hi, do you remember me?"

"Sure, what can I do for you?"

"I'm obsessed with my ex, and I can't handle it anymore. I need your help."

"Sure, I'll send you my calendar link."

She made an appointment, and after one hypnosis session, she was free of the ex.

"This is amazing, Ignacio. Why have I waited so long? Now I want a new boyfriend."

First, they do not believe what hypnosis can do; afterward, they think it's like Aladdin's lamp, just make a wish.

I said to her, "Well, not even Aladdin's lamp can make someone fall in love with you. But if you love yourself, your authentic self, somebody will fall in love with you. So let's do this. I have a program called WEB. We will do ten hypnosis and thirty coaching sessions in forty to fifty weeks working together. At the end of this program, you will be going out with a good guy."

We started the program together, and after three months, she was secure in herself, to the point that her boss noticed her more and to the point that she got an increase in her salary. Six months into the program, I noticed that she looked more attractive and happier, and I asked her. "What's happening with you?"

"I didn't want to mention it until it was more serious, but I have been dating a fantastic guy for one month."

Eight months into the program, she gets a desirable job offer within the same company, but in a different department, which concerns her because it's in another country, and she's afraid to lose her new relationship. I told her to consult her WEB and follow it. The response will be there.

During that process, she got a second increase in her salary. This one more than 30 percent because her boss noticed her move to the new department.

I have many good stories about the WEB process. I know that at first glance, it could be overwhelming. But don't worry, you're not alone! There is help available for any challenge you might be facing in your love life, parenting journey, or social interactions. The first step is to identify what type of relationship you are dealing with and then use the four levels of 'emen—your new definition of faith. I am giving you a great map here. You can feel it in your bones, This is not rocket science; this is old wisdom, and you have it inside you. I am simply a guide for your own discovery.

Chapter 8 | Have Faith in Your Financial Life

Finances and career are two things established in our minds as one with only one purpose; the acquisition and management of money. The problem is that presupposition does not bring happiness and well-being. On the contrary, it creates high levels of anxiety that result in many psychological problems.

So why do we have this pre-programmed belief in our minds? Because it served us well during the industrialized society of the last two hundred years. But, now we are moving from a physical to a mental way of working, and this shift in the production of goods and services will allow us to separate our careers and finances in a healthy, productive way. This chapter is about how you can achieve happiness and well-being by organizing your finances and your career.

In our minds, we have this presupposition that our professional careers and our finances are one and the same. We think the only way to be happy and successful in life is to sacrifice our mental or physical health in exchange for money. But that is not true. You can achieve happiness and well-being by organizing your finances and your career.

The reason it matters is that when you're happy and prosperous in your career, it reflects in your finances, and when you have financial stability, it allows you to live a happier and more productive life.

The average net worth of American families is $748,800. However, the median net worth (the typical American family's net worth of $121,700) paints a much different story. This is because many people work hard but never seem to get ahead. They are stuck in what is called the "Rat Race."

If you find yourself in this situation, there is a way out. You can take control of your finances and break free from the rat race. The traditional first step is to understand your money. How much do you make? How much do you spend? What are your debts, and what are your assets?

Start by setting some goals. Do you want to save for a down payment on a house? Do you want to retire early? Once you know what you want to achieve, you can start working toward those goals. Make a budget and stick to it. Track your progress and celebrate your successes.

This logic tells you that once you have a clear picture of your financial situation, you can make changes, and it is a good recommendation, but as you know already, the WEB strategy and the levels of 'emen are much better.

The rat race, mentioned by Robert Kiyosaki in his book *Rich Dad, Poor Dad*, is directly related to your professional career. Usually, you are forced to pick a job when you do not have any idea of what type of life you want to live, and your career is decided based on the amount of money that the activity can provide you, not the amount of happiness and well-being. Therefore, in the rat race, you must sacrifice your happiness and well-being for something far more important—money. But the funny thing, or not so funny thing, is that after many years of sacrifices to make money over happiness and well-being, your mind and body get sick; as a result, you will use all your money to heal yourself.

* * *

John had always been a successful lawyer. He was good at his job and had a thriving practice. However, over the years, John had begun to hate his job. He wasn't sure what it was, but he found himself constantly stressed out and frustrated. He would come home from work angry and irritated, taking a toll on his family life.

One day, John decided enough was enough. He was going to find a way out of the rat race. He contacted me, and we started with his WEB structure, and we discovered his passion for investing in the stock market. He had always been good with money, so he decided to invest in some stocks. He was also passionate about fixing things in his house. Why not? "Let's buy some properties and put them under an LLC and do some flipping avoiding some of the process fees." Yes, there are legal tricks where you can avoid the realtor's fee. This is the good part of my profession; you also learn things from your clients, especially from a lawyer.

It was not hard for John to redefine his career and create a new life based on his own talents and competencies. He just needed to see the situation from a different perspective and create a deep analysis of his WEB.

Do you feel like you're stuck in the rat race, struggling to make ends meet? Are you tired of working hard and not getting anywhere? If so, you're not alone. Remember, the average American family has a net worth of just $121,700.

There are many ways to escape the rat race. But these solutions are only temporary fixes. To really escape the rat race, you need to find something that you're passionate about and redefine your career or better your whole life.

If you're ready to break free from the rat race, take a serious look at your WEB. With the proper guidance, it's possible to create a new life based on your own talents and abilities.

* * *

Financial Life

What is money? What do we know about it? Where does it come from? Why do we need it? These are some questions that people have about money. Money is essential to our quality of life, but it can be perplexing. People have been taught different things about money.

Most of us are taught from a young age that money is the root of all evil. This is a belief that's common in our society. It can be challenging for people to get over this belief. I mean, it's a scary thing to think that the love of anything could be wrong.

Some people think it's wrong to love money, but we all want more money. It seems a bit odd to us that we spend so much time trying to get more money when it's not always good.

We spend a lot of time and energy working to make money. But some people think that making money is evil. They believe that wealth is associated with greed and selfishness.

Many people feel resentment toward rich people. They might feel this way because the wealthy person has a lot of things, and they might also be suspicious about how the rich person got rich. But even though many people want to be wealthy, they don't think it's okay to "take advantage of other people" to get there. But it is okay. Don't get me wrong. My rule is that you should use people for your own purposes and give them back at least ten times what they want from you. The rule is to overdeliver to others, and they will be happy to help you out.

In this segment, we will align and sharpen your faith in money. "What? Faith in money? You are a heretic, Ignacio. You're supposed to be a Christian." Yes, I am. For me, there is only one God in the form of the Father, the Son, and the Holy Spirit; and to him all honor and glory. I know that God has given me the responsibility to take care of all of his creation. Money is one of those things, so I need to have faith in my financial life. As you can see, I am changing some of my presuppositions about money, so let's start there.

Financial Life Presuppositions

I love my dad. He is a fantastic parent. I learned a lot from him. But money was not one of those things. In the beginning, it was strange to me that he didn't teach me about money when I was young. I thought, okay, he's an economist; he's supposed to know about money. Why does he resemble the Kiyosaki "Poor Dad" more than the "Rich Dad?" After studying some books about the economy, I understood the situation.

Economics studies how people use resources and what happens when there isn't enough of something—scarcity. It's all about presuppositions! He is always focused on scarcity; on the other hand, I am abundance. Boom, years of psychotherapy solved in one short phrase.

This is one of the more critical aspects of your life, as is all the WEB design. But this one is super special. A win in this area can facilitate hiring resources to simplify other areas of your WEB. Therefore pay serious attention to your presuppositions in this area and how this is affecting all your life. I recommend you read *Rich Dad Poor Dad* by Robert Kiyosaki and compare the presuppositions of each dad; you will find an interesting point of view on this.

Financial Life Vision

If you want to be rich, stop worrying about money and start worrying about the value you can add to other people. That is the key to getting rich.

If you were taught at a young age that money is a symbol of human productivity and achievement, then you understand that it's something to be respected and admired. Money is earned by people through the good things they create for each other.

What if you'd been taught that the love of money is the love of human beings and their progress? What if you'd been taught that wealth, progress, and prosperity help eliminate poverty and human suffering? That making money isn't a bad thing, but a good thing that helps others?

If you had been encouraged by everyone around you to use your talent to make money, how would your life be different now? If your children believed this, how would their lives be different?

What is your relationship with money? How much money would you like? What is your vision for your financial future?

Think about how you can achieve your goals and improve your life. Think about how you can help your loved ones and make a positive impact on society. This way, in the future, you will be able to accomplish all you want in this category. Do not limit yourself in this category; the sky's the limit.

Financial Life Purpose

Why do you want more money? What would you do with it? How would your life be different if you had more money? The purpose of having a financial vision is to make your life better. As I mentioned, money can help you use resources to impact other areas of your WEB, like staying in great physical shape, hiring professionals to shape your emotions, enjoying romantic dinners, etc. As already mentioned, one way to find good purposes in one area is to start applying the bonding and compare the purposes of different areas.

Find the real reason you want money, and the money will come to you. Do it. Find an excellent purpose for this area.

Financial Life Strategy

Making more money is something that happens in your career. Managing the money you make is something that happens in the financial category.

Many wealthy people have a solid financial plan. If you don't have an accountant or someone with financial experience, you might need help creating a plan that works for you. Actually, I would recommend you work with a professional in each area of your WEB, but especially on this one.

You need to hire someone to help you. This is one of the most important things you can do now. It can take a lot of energy to get a financial plan in place, but once you get started, it will be easier. You may not see much difference at first, but gradually your efforts will pay off.

Your bank account is going to start to grow. Your debts are going to start to disappear. It's hard to get started, but once you do, it becomes easy. And it's such a good feeling to watch this happen in your life.

Please do not wait to start this plan. Remember the famous Chinese proverb: "The best time to plant a tree was 20 years ago. The second best time is now." It's the same for your financial life, do it now.

Career

When it comes to your career, it's important to remember that passion should come before money. Money is a great motivator, but it should not be the only thing that drives you. If you are passionate about your work, the money will follow. Remember, money is just a tool. It can help you do great things, but it should not be the end goal. It's often said that money can't buy happiness. While this may be true, money can certainly help you live a happier life.

That's the reason why we need to separate the two concepts into two areas. Here please focus more on your soul's purpose. Here money is not the core. Do your best to move any money-related thing to the financial category. The focus here is on your talents and competencies and how those can serve others.

Career Presuppositions

There are many opinions about having a professional career. Some people believe it's the key to success, while others believe it's the road to failure. Many people believe that it's important to have a career, while others believe that it's more important to have a family. What do you think?

Let me share what I think. I think it's an exciting time to be alive! The era of abundance has ushered in a new way of thinking about work. No longer is it viewed as a necessary evil, but rather as a way to express our creativity and make the world a better place.

In the past, work was often seen as a way to make money. While this is still important, the focus has shifted to include other aspects, such as happiness and fulfillment. We now realize that we need to enjoy our work in order to be truly happy.

The era of abundance has also led to a renewed appreciation for our talents and abilities. We're no longer content to just do what we're told but want to use our talents to make a difference in the world. We want to feel like we're making a contribution and using our skills in the best way possible.

So what does all this mean for your career? It means that you need to find work that you are passionate about. You need to find a job that allows you to use your talents and makes you happy. The days of simply chasing money are over. Instead, focus on finding work that you love, and the money will follow.

Career Vision

So what do all these presuppositions mean for your career? It means that you need to find work that you're passionate about. You need to visualize a job that allows you to use your talents and makes you happy. The days of simply chasing money are over (old presupposition). Again, focus on finding work that you love, and the money will follow.

Imagine yourself five years from now in a job that you're passionate about. You're using your talents and making a difference in the world. You are happy, fulfilled, and doing what you love. The money is just a bonus and is there for you.

During visualization exercises, people are usually asked, "Where do you see yourself in one month from now, one year, or five years from now." And that's okay. It's a way of doing it for visualization. Now, here you will learn the reverse engineering technique to connect the vision with the strategy. "What? Are you explaining this in the last area?" Yes, in this way, you are forced to go back, do it again and do it better.

Imagine yourself five years from now in a job that you're passionate about. Then imagine yourself four years from now, three years from now, two years from now, and one year from now; you will notice that your brain is no longer guessing the strategy to achieve your vision. It is certain of each step because it already knows how to achieve it.

Career Purpose

The key to a happy life is to figure out your purpose in life and then follow it. What do you want to be when you grow up? How many times have we been asked that as a kid? It might surprise you to learn that, until recently, people couldn't even ask that question. Most ancient cultures did not give people many choices about what they could do for a job. For example, if you were born in ancient Sparta, you would have to do the job assigned to you.

You have this amazing opportunity to shape your career based on your purpose. This category is driven by your desires, your passion, and your deepest needs. Go wild on this. Free your creativity. Free your emotions. Allow yourself to express yourself and forget about the idea that a career is for your whole life. As a kid, I always wanted to be a firefighter, and I did it for some years, and I moved on. I wanted to learn about computers. I did some years of system engineering, and I moved on. I wanted to be a psychologist. I did it, and I moved on. Even though nobody understood the purpose of all my actions, all those actions had a purpose, bringing me to where I am today. Follow your purpose, and it will take you to your happiness and well-being.

Career Strategy

It's a lot better to live in a smaller house, drive a lesser automobile, dress less expensively, and be delighted than to be unhappy at work.

So it's time for you to go out there and discover the perfect job for you. But that's easier said than done, right?

I've been poor and homeless, and I can tell you that I would rather be happy on a modest income than rich and miserable any day. In 2005, I was living in a nice apartment in Paris with my cousin. But I decided to live on the streets of Paris while studying for my master's degree just to be happy and free. And I would do it again if needed.

I was a highly-paid professional in my native Venezuela, and I never sold my soul to bribery or for easy money. I resigned, and for the first year in Canada, I worked as a pharmacy cashier.

In Canada, I was instructed to modify an ergonomic report on a job position by the lawyers of a major corporation, but I informed them that it was one I had completed and that I could produce a new one to see if I was correct. Furthermore, to collaborate, I could invite an external consultant to the study. But I would not alter my report as demanded by a group of attorneys to suit the company's interests. That job position was causing damage to the workers, and that was my professional analysis. As a result, I lost my employment but not my happiness and well-being.

The question is, what are you going to do about it? Take a look at your career vision. How much emotional salary do you want to make? How much material salary do you want to make? Do you currently have a job that can help you reach your goal? Is there anything that you could do to make it happen? Do you enjoy what you do for a living? Is this something that matters to you on an emotional level? If not, what are your plans going forward? Are you good at what you do? Can you become better at it?

Take a look at your career vision and use the reverse engineering method to tie it to the plan. I generally utilize a hypnosis technique in this area with my clients, and it's critical that you feel all the elements of the experience in your future, five years from now. Be there, feel it with all your senses, and ask yourself how to get to this point.

Take a look at all the events in that five-year period. Now come back. What did you do last month, last year, and the previous two years up until your present? See how all these events connect to your present? It's like magic: you'll have a road map from here to your future. And it's true; some days will be like an excellent highway, while others will be like a bumpy road. But do not worry about that bumpy road ahead; you will need to make difficult decisions regarding the process, but you will be satisfied since you already know where you're going.

The Era of Abundance

For the first time in history, humanity is now rich with a plethora of resources. We have a large number of commodities on hand. The problem is that we don't know how to utilize it. This wealth has significant social, economic, and political implications.

Humans have resorted to dieting for the first time in millions of years during their evolutionary journey. Dieting isn't just limited to food; it also applies to various other behaviors, such as television, video games, traveling, sex, and drugs. Take a look at Johnny Depp's life; he requires a diet of many things.

We're seeing the imminent death of the false god called Economy because the economy is the science of handling scarcity—no scarcity, no economy. How are people reacting, and how do our political leaders respond to this abundance?

From the left, they want to increase government regulations and reduce production capacity to recreate a scarcity-controlled state. From the right, they create an imaginary scarcity. The marketing machinery always creates the new goal you need to achieve, and every time you reach that goal, you have a new one. Because of the existence of this new virtual scarcity, the marketing machinery is hypnotizing people to increase the base of Maslow's pyramid. In this way, you cannot achieve the top levels of love, belonging, self-esteem, and self-actualization.

The top of this political plan is a mix of authoritarian capitalism. A total control of the resources from the state and a powerful marketing machinery that hypnotizes people to increase the base of Maslow's hierarchy of needs. I know it firsthand. It's the way the government does it in Venezuela. And for many years, I had a personal problem with politics but not anymore because I understand Maistre's quote, "Every nation gets the government it deserves."

These days I just want each individual that comes to my practice to reach their God-given purpose, and to do that, in my first book, I presented a simple solution for this problem, Segovia's Tower of Needs. The basic idea is that you need to transform your pyramid of needs into a tower. Having the same volume of needs in each level will allow you to move to the next level. Not only that, it will enable you to move without restrictions up and down, allowing you to enjoy the present state because you are not sacrificing one for another. This concept was presented by Jesus. It was the idea of poverty, which we call minimalist nowadays, but people didn't interpret it properly.

"Then he looked up at his disciples and said: 'Blessed are you who are poor, for yours is the kingdom of God. Blessed are you who are hungry now, for you will be filled. Blessed are you who weep now, for you will laugh." Luke 6:20–21 (NRSV)

The famous Stanford marshmallow experiment proved in 1972 that delayed gratification or deferred gratification will give you success. And for me, it is clear, not only in this life but in the next one too. As simple as that. Your human freedom nowadays, especially in the two areas in this chapter, depends directly on your capacity to manage your deferred gratification.

I won't go deep on this because you'll notice this effect on the B (bond) part of the WEB.

To be successful, one must be able to resist temptation and delay gratification. This was certainly the case for John D. Rockefeller, one of the most successful businessmen in American history.

Rockefeller was born in 1839 during a time of great opportunity and wealth in America. He was raised by parents who taught him the importance of hard work and delayed gratification. As a young man, Rockefeller worked long hours in his father's business, eventually starting his own business at the age of twenty-four.

Rockefeller's success was due, in part, to his ability to delay gratification and focus on his long-term goals. He was willing to work hard now to enjoy greater rewards later on. Rockefeller once said, "I always tried to live so that my life would be worth living." This focus on purpose and long-term goals is what allowed him to achieve such great success.

Although you don't have to make Rockefeller sacrifices in this abundance era, if you combine some of this delayed gratification with your faith in the financial and career realms, you will notice how the magic begins to occur in your life. All of this is similar to going to the gym; all you have to do is go. You begin one day slowly, with discomfort, and after a few weeks, it transforms into a habit that is unconsciously woven into your everyday routine. Simply just do it and repeat it again and again.

Chapter 9 | Bonding Strategies

"He who controls others may be powerful, but he who has mastered himself is mightier still." —Lao Tzu

I feel part of a futuristic movie; I see my oldest cousin Cheche and his friends connecting cables. They have four computers in one office, and they want to share information. Imagine sending data from one computer to another? That's amazing. It's the summer of 1987, and my cousin is explaining that it's already possible, but he's learning how to do it.

I had the opportunity to experience firsthand the development of computers during the eighties because I spent a lot of time at Cheche's house; my cousin was learning about system engineering at Metropolitan University—the same university and the same career I entered into in 1996.

I studied six semesters of system engineering before changing careers to psychology; I realized that my talents were more helpful in cleaning viruses off people's minds than computers.

But all my experience in that career was not in vain. I was well trained in decision analysis. Therefore, using simple tools like a decision tree, influence diagram, or more complex ones like a Bayesian network was beneficial in understanding people's behavior.

It's not necessary to use weird names for what I'll explain here. For example, after the creation of the World Wide Web, it's much simpler to explain a hypertext or hyperlink.

So what is hypertext or hyperlink? It's a command that calls for information. For example, in the song "Hickety, Pickety, Bumblebee," the teacher calls for a child to say their name. The teacher invites everyone to say the name, "Let's say it." After the kids say the name, the teacher says, "Let's clap it." In this case, the teacher controls the action.

In a modified game version, the teacher calls the kid's name first, and the first kid performs the next step. Then this kid passes leadership to the second kid. In this way, the leadership of the game passes from one kid to another, similar to when you pass from one page to another on the internet. But the internet is infinite, so you don't know why you're on that Facebook page at some point!

If you go deeper into technicalities, a hypertext contains text linked to other information. In hyperlinks, the references are used in hypertext or with other hypermedia. Hypertext involves only text. A hyperlink involves text, media, audio, video, images, and graphics. But that's not important here. The critical part is the connection between them (Bond) and the idea that you are capable of calling up certain information that's kept on a server W (World) or server E (Essence).

And this is not a new concept to be applied to people's lives. For example, the idea of hyperlinking (Bond) wisdom to how we think, feel, and behave is a common variable in the first clear hyperlink book in human history, The Bible.

In October 2007, Pastor Christoph Römhild and Chris Harrison, an associate professor of human-computer interaction at Carnegie Mellon University, created a dataset of cross-references found in the Bible, finding 63,779 cross-references in total.

You can find the full-color image at https://www.chrisharrison. net/index.php/Visualizations/BibleViz

The WEB works in the same way. The WEB methodology functions as a process that asks questions of my client inside the W-E areas. These areas need to refer to one another for information before a decision is executed by the person.

It sounds a little robotic-oriented at the beginning, but let me tell you, it's not a tool that will enslave you after you set it up and you have it on hand. On the contrary, you will feel totally free for the first time in your life.

During the WEB process, I always ask my clients to think about what's more important in their life—physical, mental, emotional, character, etc. The WEB is all about you, about what you really want in life. It's a manual of discipline to achieve your perfect life.

Well-Being Theory (WBT)

As you already know, we are bonding—putting everything together in this chapter.

So let's go back to our initial promises—happiness and well-being. Why do I always talk about these two together?

My clients come to me when they're down in the dumps because their job is a source of much stress, or they're not getting along with their roommates or family, or they don't like where they live. They come to see me because they want to be happy. None of them ask for well-being. They ask for happiness. And I believe you want happiness. For sure, that's the main reason you're here, but true happiness is really about your well-being. That's the real treasure of this book.

Abraham Maslow, in 1943, was one of the first psychologists to coin the term "well-being," which he defined as a person who has achieved self-actualization. The concept of self-actualization was a precursor to the PERMA model, which describes features of a flourishing person, and the Well-Being Theory (WBT), which provides the primary theoretical support to this book.

In his inaugural address as the incoming president of the American Psychological Association in 1998, Dr. Martin Seligman redirected attention away from mental illness and pathology to focusing on what is beneficial and wonderful in life. This should sound familiar to you.

(-5)—(-4)—(-3)—(-2)—(-1)—(+1)—(+2)—(+3)—(+4)—(+5)

From that point on, various research and theories have been conducted to examine the positive psychology techniques that aim to make life worth living and how to define, quantify, and create well-being.

Seligman's theory was designed to help people better manage their lives and achieve more happiness. He selected five components that individuals pursue because they are inherently appealing and contribute to well-being. These aspects are followed for their own sake and are defined and assessed independently of one another.

The five components (PERMA; Seligman, 2012) are:

- Positive emotion
- Engagement
- Relationships
- Meaning
- Accomplishments

Positive Emotion

Happiness, in and of itself, is only one component of positive emotion. Positive emotions include hope, interest, joy, love, compassion, pride, amusement, and gratitude. Positive feelings indicate flourishing and can be cultivated or developed to enhance well-being.

Positive emotions may help individuals develop habitual thinking and behavior by allowing them to explore, savor, and integrate positive feelings into daily life. In addition, the beneficial effects of good feelings can counteract the damaging effects of negative emotions, increasing resilience.

The following are some ways to create positive emotions:

- Spend quality time with people you care about.
- Love yourself, your kids, and your friends.
- Participate in activities that you enjoy physically, mentally, or emotionally.
- Examine your blessings—what's going well in your life— and your spirituality.

Engagement

The term "flow" was coined by Mihály Csíkszentmihályi in the late 1970s. Flow is a state of being fully immersed in an activity. It might be defined as living in the present moment and focusing exclusively on the task. Flow, or the notion of engagement, occurs when an ideal mix of challenge and skill/strength is discovered.

When people utilize their best personality traits, they are more likely to have flow. After six months, individuals who tried to apply their talents in innovative ways each day for a week were happier and less depressed than those who did not. The idea of engagement is much more significant than simply "being happy," but happiness is one of the many benefits of engagement.

The following are some ways to create engagement:

- Participate in activities you genuinely enjoy, and time will fly during them.
- Despite everything, remember to keep practicing living in the moment every now and then.

- Identify and understand your character's strengths, then pursue activities you enjoy. "Where did I read about this? Oh yes, there's something about this in our essence analysis!"

Relationships

The various connections people have with others, such as their partners, friends, family members, coworkers, bosses/mentors/supervisors, and the community at large, are considered relationships. Feeling supported, cherished, and valued by others is referred to as a relationship in the PERMA model.

The model accounts for relationships because humans are naturally social beings. This can be seen in every area of life, but social ties become especially vital as we grow older. For example, the social setting is essential in preventing cognitive decline, and crucial social networks aid in better physical health among the elderly.

Many people desire to strengthen their ties with family and friends. For example, sharing good news or celebrating an achievement has been shown in studies to promote solid bonds and better relationships. Furthermore, demonstrating interest in others, particularly in close or intimate relationships, increases intimacy, well-being, and happiness.

Ways to create positive relationships:

Just check your W; you have a personalized formula to do this already.

Meaning

Another fundamental human characteristic is the desire for significance and value. People need to feel valued and worthy. Belonging and/or serving something greater than oneself is defined as having a purpose in life. It allows individuals to focus on what matters most during tremendous struggle or adversity.

For every person, finding significance or purpose in life is unique. Finding meaning may be done through a career, a social or political cause, a creative activity, or a religious/spiritual belief. In addition, a profession, extracurricular volunteering, or community activities might provide it.

Personal beliefs and goals are based on a feeling of purpose, and individuals who believe in a cause have more life satisfaction and fewer health issues.

The following are some ways to create meaning in your life:

• First, pay attention to the purpose descriptions in each area of your W-E.

• If you are low in meaning, pay attention to your legacy in your career, kids, or spiritual life.

Accomplishments

Last but not least, this is an essential component.

In PERMA, accomplishment, achievement, mastery, or competence are all terms that have been used to describe success. A feeling of accomplishment results from striving for and achieving objectives, mastering a project, and having the self-motivation to finish what you started out to do. This contributes to one's mental health since individuals take pleasure in their life's accomplishments.

The keywords for this concept include effort, diligence, and zest to achieve objectives. However, when the aim is to accomplish anything with an internal desire or for the sake of searching for improvement, well-being and flourishing are possible compared to external goals such as money, fame, or Instagram standards.

Achieving intrinsic targets (such as growth and connection) generates more significant health benefits. That's the main reason for the planning aspect of each W-E area; to guarantee your personal, intrinsic success.

Ways to create accomplishments:

- If you are at +1, start with SMART Goals (Specific, Measurable, Achievable, Relevant, and Time-Bound).
- If you are at +3, go for a "bee hag" (BHAG–Big Hairy Audacious Goal).
- Consider your prior successes.
- Look for innovative methods to commemorate your accomplishments.

At the end of this book, you'll find the measurement link for PERMA, and you'll receive two results from your online PERMA test:

Your total well-being score ranging from 1 (low well-being) to 10 (high well-being)

(-5)—(-4)—(-3)—(-2)—(-1)—(+1)—(+2)—(+3)—(+4)—(+5) WEB Stats

(1 | 2 | 3 | 4 | 5 | 6 | 7 | 8 | 9 | 10) PERMA Well-Being Score

Your negativity scores ranging from 1 (low negativity) to 10 (high negativity)

(-5)—(-4)—(-3)—(-2)—(-1)—(+1)—(+2)—(+3)—(+4)—(+5) WEB Stats

(10 | 9 | 8 | 7 | 6 | 5 | 4 | 3 | 2 | 1) PERMA Negativity Scores

Don't worry about this now. We'll do the numbers in the evaluation area. For now, let's continue with the bonding.

Bonding with *The 7 Habits of Highly Effective People*

We have the WEB formula thus far. The W is the World, the E is the Essence, and the B is the Bond between all system components. Now we'll tie that in with the seven habits tactic.

Dr. Stephen Covey developed the seven habits to move from dependence to independence and then to interdependency, forming a connection inside yourself and with others.

His book's first chapter begins with a description of how many people who have achieved a high level of outward success continue to suffer from an inner need to enhance their personal effectiveness and develop good relationships with others.

According to Covey, we view the world entirely based on our perceptions. We must alter ourselves to change a particular scenario and be able to modify our views to do so (our premises).

Covey discovered that a significant shift in how people define success has occurred over 200 years. The foundation of success in previous times was character ethics (such as integrity, humility, fidelity, temperance, bravery, justice, patience, industry, simplicity, and modesty). But starting around the 1920s, people's perceptions of success changed to what Covey calls "personality ethic" (where success is determined by personality, image, attitudes, and actions). That means before the 1920s, success was based on the E. After that, we focused on the W.

E and the First Three Habits

The first three habits are:

1. Be Proactive

We are typically reactive to everything that happens in our lives. We suffer from an issue and seek to fix it. When we are harmed, we want to retaliate and defend ourselves. That is a reactive lifestyle. It's our natural state. It's linked to our reptilian brain, which is fundamental to us and enables us to react.

It's evident that being reactive is not beneficial to people at this time in our history. When we only react to events, we always get into more trouble. That method was created for emergency situations, including those of life and death, but not for everyday problems.

We must be proactive in dealing with daily scenarios. We must plan ahead.

That's what we're doing with the WEB system. We're planning ahead of the responses that we'll have in each situation. So the whole WEB system is proactive. It's a way to set up the policies and procedures of your own company and establish those for the moment when you'll need them later.

One of the phrases stuck in my brain from *The 7 Habits of Highly Effective People* is the phrase attributed to Viktor Frankl; "Between stimulus and response, there is a space. In that space is our power to choose our response. In our response lies our growth and our freedom."

And when you develop your E (Essence), you'll see the data space grow and grow, but it's not an empty space. That space needs to be filled by our WEB system. That space must be filled by the four levels of each area of your life. Every time you decide anything based on your WEB policies and procedures, you will obtain the results you want. However, if you just react, the results are gambling. Maybe you'll receive the results you want, but there is a high possibility that you will receive adverse outcomes. It's like casino gambling.

2. Begin with the End in Mind

The second habit in Covey's book begins with the end in mind. During the WEB exercise, you found your vision in each area of your life. In each section of your WEB system, you established your vision. By now, you should have a full general vision of your life, and if you put together each section of the web system in your vision, you'll have a broad vision of your life. You'll see your future, the quality of life you want, and the happiness and well-being you want.

3. Put First Things First

Quoting Dr. J. Roscoe Miller, former U.S. President Dwight D. Eisenhower, in a 1954 speech to the Second Assembly of the World Council of Churches, said:

"I have two kinds of problems: the urgent and the important. The urgent are not important, and the important are never urgent."

It's been said that Eisenhower managed his workload and priorities using this principle. He recognized that excellent time management necessitates being successful as well as efficient. To put it another way, we must spend our time on important things rather than those that are merely urgent.

To do so, we need to understand the distinction:

Important: Activities that help us achieve our goals. E oriented.

Urgent: Activities that demand immediate attention usually involve achieving

someone else's goals. W oriented.

It's essential to know which activities are important and which are urgent so we can focus on the important ones and not be distracted by the urgent but unimportant ones. This way, we can move our businesses and careers forward instead of just putting out fires.

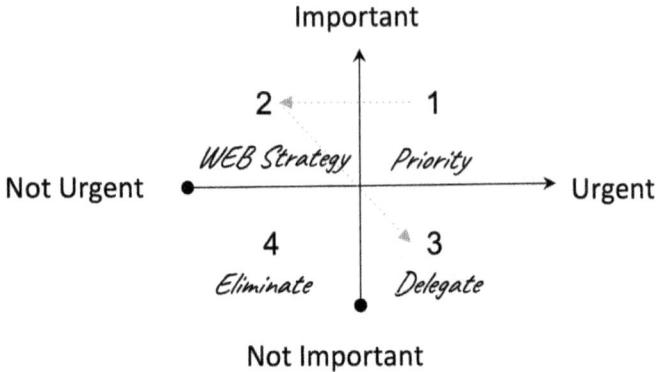

Important

2	1
WEB Strategy	*Priority*

Not Urgent ●————————→ **Urgent**

4	3
Eliminate	*Delegate*

Not Important

The most essential quadrant for your WEB is the second one, where you have the important but not urgent things. All the parts of your web system are important but not urgent. If you do not plan ahead or are irresponsible with your second quadrant, the important things will turn urgent, and the second quadrant will transform into your first quadrant. You should maintain all in your second quadrant, but I understand that life happens, and sometimes you will have urgent and important things, but do not make this the norm; it is an exception; quadrant one should be empty all the time.

You should have a list of things in the second quadrant. A list that should come from your WEB system, especially from the strategy—your plan. Every step of your plan should be here, in small activities, constant small positive changes that can result in major and more significant growth of your WEB, which sits in the second quadrant. In the first quadrant, we have what is important and urgent. If you ignore your second quadrant, you'll start to have factors here and set yourself up simply for reactions.

The third quadrant is the space for the urgent but not important. In this quadrant are all the requirements from others that haven't been negotiated on your W. As you already know, you should come to the W to give to others and participate in others' lives. However, during your W analysis, you established the factors you'll bring to the table for others; you'll bring your offerings. But it's clear that those offerings are sometimes part of other people's requirements, and sometimes people will demand more from you. The third quadrant is home to other people's demands outside your W. Delegate those activities to others. Your happiness and well-being will be compromised if you lose all your resources in this quadrant when you pass to your W area without knowing your essence.

Usually, you live in this quadrant because you don't have personal things to defend. You don't have individual requirements to bring to the table. You have demands from others; your work; your family; your friends; and the economy. This is a dangerous place to live, but it's not as risky as the fourth quadrant.

The fourth quadrant is not important, not urgent things. You should not be here. For example, when you're spending time looking at pictures on Instagram or TikTok, you could be doing something important. Without a WEB system, people get easily stuck in this quadrant. I'm not saying you shouldn't take some time for relaxation or have a vacation. But that resting time should be part of your WEB system. You should have it in your WEB strategy if it's crucial for you. Any relaxation trips, cruises, walking in the park, or playing with your dog, are important. So they should be in your important, not urgent quadrant.

But you shouldn't be doing it if it's not giving you anything in your WEB system. You shouldn't be looking at or sharing TikTok videos without any reason. You will have a purpose there if you have a business that should be promoted on TikTok or Instagram. Then you have a reason; you have a strategy. You have all your faith levels in that activity on TikTok, Instagram, and Facebook. That's okay because it's an important thing to do for you. Remember, I'm not telling you what's important or not for you here. You're designing your own life. The significant thing here is that you realize that the activity you're doing is important for you.

If you're doing an activity that's not important or urgent for YOU, you need to stop right now.

If you do all this and repeat these three habits from Covey's strategy, you'll move from dependency to independence. You'll see a new life and perceive yourself and the things around you differently. This will give you the tools to develop a better W.

W and the Next Three Habits

We are passing from independency to interdependency, and Covey explains to us here three different habits:

4. Think Win-Win

Win-win is a way of thinking that sees life as a cooperative arena, not a competitive one. In this way of thinking, everyone can benefit from agreements or solutions that are mutually beneficial and satisfying.

I'm not talking about the nonsense when, during our career or playing a soccer game, everybody receives a winning medal. At the game, we all play, improve our bodies, have a good time with our friends, and experience mutual benefit in that human interaction. Not everybody wins the trophy, but everybody receives a benefit.

This is the primary importance of bringing your E to the negotiation table. The most important thing for you is your E—not a medal, not a trophy. Don't get distracted by external recognition. At the negotiation table, you need to defend your E and fulfill as much as possible the other person's E.

In this part, you'll seek to achieve your E and the other's E; first in your love relationship; second in your legacy, with your kids, or your nephews, etc., and then in your family, friends, career, and finances.

In all those areas, you need to negotiate with other people. Next, you'll see that you must communicate your E to others. The fourth habit, Think Win-Win, teaches us to pay attention to other people's E and what other people put forward when entering a relationship.person's

5. Seek First to Understand, Then to Be Understood

Most people want to be understood. When you want to get your point across, you might do any of the following: completely ignore the other person; pretend to listen; only hear certain parts of the conversation, or focus on the words being said without understanding their meaning. This happens because most people listen with the intent of replying, not to understand. In addition, people usually prepare what they will say in their minds while listening. This makes it difficult to understand what the other person is saying.

To influence other people, you need to find out what they want. You need to listen carefully to them and understand their thoughts and feelings. Pay attention to their words and body language to get a complete understanding. Once you have done this, people will start trusting your opinions and advice.

Napoleon Hill's book *The Law of Success* teaches us that the way to influence others is to help them achieve what they want. So if you want to be a leader in your life and impact those around you, you need to know what they want.

People often don't know what they want. To figure out what other people want, you need to listen to what they say and what they don't say. When you listen to people, they notice and pay attention to your needs. Listening is a two-way street that can create a positive relationship. It's like magic!

6. Synergize

When people interact and are open to each other's influence, they can come up with new ideas. This is because of the differences in their backgrounds and experiences.

And when people work together, they can produce better results than if they worked separately. This is called synergy. Synergy is when the whole is greater than the sum of the parts. For example, two plus two equals four, but when added together, two plus two can also equal six.

Synergizing is the habit of creative cooperation. This means that people work together to find new solutions to old problems. This doesn't happen on its own but is a process. People with different personal experiences and expertise bring all this to the table to help make this possible.

So now you're working hard to achieve your and the other person's goals. You can do this by bonding your E with the W. The only way to do that is to interconnect each level of faith, each level of 'emen, with each other. That means you need to connect your four levels of 'emen with the other person.

And sometimes, you'll need to help the other person understand their faith, to understand their four levels of 'emen in the different sections of their E and their W before you can achieve synergy. Again, some people don't know anything about their faith. They don't know anything about their E or their W. You need to help them understand, but you're not a therapist. You can only help them understand up to a certain point. Then they'll be able to understand your goals and how you want to connect with them. They'll also realize that this will help them in return.

The final habit is about constantly improving yourself.

7. Sharpen the Saw

Sharpen the saw if you want to keep sawing. You need to keep using the same tools, but you also need to keep them sharp. This means you have to work on yourself and ensure you are continually learning and growing.

The woodcutter's experience shared by Covey in his book goes something like this;

> A youngster nearby asked, "What are you doing?" as the woodcutter strained to saw down a tree.
>
> "Are you blind?" the woodcutter challenged. "I'm sawing down this tree."
>
> The young man was unrepentant. "You appear exhausted! Take a break."
>
> The woodcutter told the young man that he'd been sawing for hours and couldn't afford to stop.
>
> "If you sharpen the saw," the youngster countered, "you'll be able to cut down the tree much faster."
>
> "I don't have time to sharpen the saw," the woodcutter said. "Don't you see that I'm too busy?"

We need to sharpen our E, and we need to sharpen our W. Then we need to sharpen our WEB strategy. After we sharpen that strategy, we need to bond it.

You need to interconnect your essence components—physical, mental, emotional, character, and spiritual. You need to bond first before you go into the world. After you're ready with your essence, you can renegotiate your relationship with your partner or loved one. You can renegotiate your relationship with your kids, your father, your mother, your family, your friends, and the people close to you.

You can change your financial and career circumstances if you so desire. In that way, the cash and your professional aspirations may be met. Fulfill the potential within you. This is a crucial aspect of the bonding chapter because it emphasizes how we must discover who we are. Learning everything in this book and doing it repeatedly will provide you with a sharp saw.

Chapter 10 | It Really Works!

Life is as simple as *Dora the Explorer*, but for some reason, we prefer to move from, say, a simple life in nature to New York and experience a tragedy/comedy with some friends.

It's exciting to consider the possibilities when a client asks you, "Do you teach this? I'd like to assist others in the same manner that you assisted me." This is a clear indication of someone in +3 who is ready to give back to those around them.

Yes, it's true that not everyone reaches this stage; in reality, it's less than 20 percent. I learned to accept the fact that not all my clients reach this step. They came to accomplish something, to overcome a problem. So yes, it's true, but there is much more to life than simply leaping from problem to problem; you already know that.

And, as always, it's the Pareto principle at work. In a similar way, less than 20 percent of those who buy this book will read these lines, so congratulations on being among those who have a genuine opportunity to achieve happiness and well-being.

You already know that the true meaning of life isn't to fix all your difficulties in order to be happy. This is reactionary, and you are a proactive individual.

You should now focus on living your plan every day since you have a strategy in each area of your life. And life happens; I'm sure you've experienced that yourself. But let me tell you a secret: God will not ask if you missed the mark or not; he'll inquire whether you aim at it constantly. A wonderful father is overjoyed when his child takes the right path forward.

It's okay if you just take the first step; at least take the time to find your faith in your physical area. Just find the four levels of 'emen in your body, and ask yourself, what is the real deal with my body? (Your presuppositions, vision, purpose, and plan.) And do it. You'll see significant changes in your life just by focusing on one area.

But you know that by acting on all of them holistically, big things will happen. All the PERMA factors will show up on each day of your life, and that will provide you with the happiness you seek in your life.

In the first chapter, we agreed that success in life is defined as success in daily experiences, and you can shape those daily experiences for you.

I promised you happiness and well-being, not the "happiness" found in seeking the holy grail. I promised to help you to the next level of happiness and well-being on a simple scale with simple numbers. Do you recall where you were there?

I'm sure, at the beginning of this book, you had a very different paradigm—a very different presupposition about happiness and well-being. Just that change alone is a very big gain in your life.

Many of my clients come as a result of some issue, difficulty, or grief that's affecting them significantly in their lives. People also come to my therapy sessions as a result of being put on my route by life.

I had a client who brought his girlfriend to our session. She was experiencing anxiety, depression, stress, and maybe bipolar disorder, according to him. I told him that I'd see her just because he wanted me to, but my focus was not on psychopathologies; rather, it was on human potential. They were originally from

Venezuela, so I thought it'd be great if we could all work together to assist them. But I was almost sure she wasn't yet ready for what lay ahead of her.

After the first session, we discovered that she was not yet ready for it. However, Joe got caught in the middle of my approach to working on this process of a life design. He decided that as he couldn't assist her, he'd like to work on his own development. So he began collaborating with me. Finally, after almost a year, he was prepared to take charge of his own life by writing his life guide and undertaking projects.

And I keep a wonderful friendship with Joe. Coaching and hypnosis gave me one of the advantages over psychotherapy, which I didn't have previously: to maintain a strong relationship with my clients.

After a few years, Joe decided to bring his family from Venezuela here. But they didn't have the documents, so they walked across the frontier and sought asylum.

That process is complicated for people. The South Mexican-United States frontier is challenging, especially when they're arrested and taken through the whole process of asylum.

After a few months in the United States, Joe sent his sister to see me. She was highly anxious, depressed, and stressed. She had also suffered an injury and could not work or do various activities.

We started by addressing fundamental levels of anxiety, such as primary concerns. Let's call her Olivia. Olivia was so terrified of various things that she could not complete basic daily activities. A few methods were used to reduce the anxiety gradually, and afterward, I started working with Olivia on this program.

The changes were tremendous. The changes in her life and her relationship had gone from one extreme to the other. She explained to me that how she was feeling, the things she was enjoying, and how she was looking at life at this point were all entirely new for her. She said that in the last fifteen years, she had not been living at all.

Olivia had been fleeing from her problems. And since we began working on this project, she has been able to move from a pessimistic stream to the point where she appears to be living in a different way. She was ready to reclaim more of her life once she reached the zero mark on our scale. But that's not all; she was also determined to build her future in America.

Nowadays, she moves between zero and one. Sometimes she has glimpses of minus one. But Olivia lived for many years in the minus two area. And that's so different. For her, the difference of two to three digits is a new life. It's a new life that's giving her hope and strength to build a future for her future generations.

If you are a professional in this area and want to help others grow in their personal development, you should know that it's very gratifying to see people's lives change.

Of course, seeking asylum to enjoy life in another country is not a common scenario, but this example is important because usually, these types of situations in life push us to recreate our life.

In those cases, it's easy to see the broad picture I'm trying to paint with this book. On the other hand, when you're at ease in your job, life, and marriage, a substantial change isn't required. But do not take your life for granted. Perhaps you need some fine-tuning here and there, and this process will assist you in doing so. But, for many of my clients, a life transformation is essential, and a new life is crucial.

Immigration allowed me to assist individuals in redefining their lives. Newly arrived people make up 12 percent of the population of the United States. So this book will be ideal for them.

Perhaps you know individuals who are altering their lives because they are changing careers, divorcing, or simply want to change their lives because they are unfulfilled in their current life. This book is for them.

This book will help anybody who wants to find their life's deep roots to achieve amazing things.

Another client, Samantha, came to me because she was having trouble with her ex-boyfriend. She was torn by his presence in the gym and their shared interests. And, in some ways, she was compulsive about this ex-boyfriend. She wanted to alter what had gone wrong with her relationship with him and all of her previous boyfriends.

Samantha is a highly successful working woman in her forties with a great life, yet she has personal difficulties and problems with failure. And she came to address that issue about her ex-boyfriend. We began looking at several aspects of her life, and I recommended that she utilize this program to help her build herself up, be more confident, start to shine, and become less of an object of comparison for men.

Based on her experience in her childhood, she had a personal view of a relationship where the woman was very dependent on the man—not financially but more emotionally. And we started working on this live project. At that moment, she was single but looking for a partner. So I told her that when she grew in her essence and rebuilt her inner self, that partner would appear.

So we started working on her essence. And when we were working on her character, someone appeared, and she asked me what to do. Samantha said she never knew this person was interested in her, and now he was calling her and inviting her to go out. I told her that she could start checking out that relationship but to first finish the five levels of essence.

And she said she would start going out with him for dinner, etc., and focus on and finish the five levels of essence.

After a couple of months, after we got into the love relationship area and began working on her world areas, Samantha told me she needed my help and opinion about the situation with her new partner.

This was a great moment for some personal wisdom. With a big smile and saying to myself, "YES!" I opened her project book. Because my clients pay for the whole package, they get access to a website application where they have their notes, and I started reading her notes to her without telling her. "Well, you should do this. It would be best if you do this. You should..."

And suddenly, she noticed. "Hey, are you reading my notes?"

"Sure, I'm reading your notes because this is your live project. In these notes, you have your policies and procedures. You now have a company called Samantha. Your person is a corporation, and you've already written your company's vision, mission, policies, and procedures. You need to follow them. I don't have the responses for your life. You have the answers for your life. So you need to go back and read it."

And she was amazed. She was amazed by this simple fact. She was amazed because now she had a guide. Finally, she has her own guidance on decisions she needs to make in her life without depending on me to tell her what to do.

I always tell my students, "Your goal is to graduate your client. They need to be able to be independent. You are just a temporary guide for your client." And this book is precisely that—a guide, and you decide how to use it.

I recommend two ways to use it. First, go fully immersed. Read the book every six months, do the evaluations, and review your life project. The second option is to just focus on your body. Do the same only for your physical health area and see what happens. In any of those cases, you can contact me at worklifebalancedoesntwork.com. We offer a limited number of free strategy sessions per week (schedule permitting) to help as many people as we can. I do this whenever I have new graduates at the school to pick clients for them. If you don't have the budget to go into a full project with me, I can refer you to one of my students. This is a great deal for you and for them because I supervise all the cases anyway.

Chapter 11 | Now What?

"So I say to you: Ask and it will be given to you; seek and you will find; knock and the door will be opened to you."—Luke 11:9 (NIV)

Okay, maybe when you first picked up this book, you wondered about your work-life balance. Initially, you were unsure what this guy was implying with the notion that "work-life balance" doesn't work. You may have said, "I require it. I need a work-life balance or a basic strategy for achieving happiness and well-being. That's something I need. Happiness and well-being are things I require."

And now you are more clear about these things. You know why work-life balance doesn't work, why well-being and happiness are interconnected, and why you should not separate them. And how by finding well-being and the PERMA factors in your life, you will achieve happiness as a by-product of that. So now you know, you don't need to wonder anymore.

You're crystal clear about this pledge from the start of this book. You're aware of these five phases you must go through in order to succeed. You know how to transition from a negative aspect on this continuum of minus five to a positive area. It's clear that life changes all the time, and you must be prepared for it.

You know that if you maintain your plus one or plus two, you are not close to that border of mental illness, even physical or spiritual illness. On the other hand, if you are in that negative five or negative four areas, you understand a little more about the need for clinical psychology, a psychotherapist, or psychiatric support medication.

And if you are struggling with life around negative three (and you can clearly now see where you are and where you want to be), following these five simple steps will change your paradigm from the work-life balance to the world essence bonding the WEB. Step 1, making the decision of shifting paradigms. Step 2, you just find the four levels of your 'emen in any activity of your life. You've got ten different areas, but you can use that formula for anything in your life or anything you want to find some faith in. What do you want in life instead?

Step 3, well, use your essence. Cover your five essence areas; your body, thinking process, emotions, character, and spirituality. Then in Step 4, you can go into the world on solid ground. You can now have your policies and procedures in your essence and negotiate with the world. Now you don't need to depend on people to say what you are or to identify you as this or that.

Now you know who you are, and you have a document to go and negotiate with your partner, family, and friends. In that way, they will know who you are, who you really are. In Step 5, you just bond the strategies and interconnect your essence, your world, and restart it again and again.

Bond all those areas, and you create a habit that you can put into a cycle of active improvement. You can use this book and your personal book as live support every six months or even just once a year.

You can review your book. But, remember, every time you review your book, you should do it with a calm mind. Don't review your book in difficult times.

You should plan ahead to do this review. It's not that you will change the book every time or that you will need to accommodate certain situations in your life. The idea of the policies and procedures for your life is to have a guide. And this guidance can only be reviewed every six months or every year, and as time passes, you will see that it will be more permanent.

And I have shared with you that I had difficult moments in some parts of my life. But now I can tell you how my story is at present. I'm living right now in what I call my paradise. I live in a house that I love. Not only that, the house is surrounded by the things I always wanted.

A couple of blocks from my house is a kung fu academy. I always wanted to practice martial arts, but for many reasons, I didn't have the opportunity. We have almost four years of practicing kung fu in an amazing academy called Nee's Kung Fu, where my kids do their after-school training every day. We love it, and we are already black belts.

I have a church close to me that's called Potential Church. And its mission is to help people achieve their God's potential. Do you think it's a coincidence that now I have a community that's totally aligned with my values, with the dreams I've been working on ever since I can remember?

They align with all the values I learned in my studies as a psychologist for my master's degree. And they are just a couple of blocks from my house. I have an academy where I'm teaching all this knowledge to other people so they can help the Hispanic community in a massive way. I help my clients, we have a beautiful life, and I'm grateful for this.

I'm grateful to God because he guided me to achieve all these things. And I don't believe this is the end. I believe there is much more I can do for my family, friends, and the Hispanic community. So I'm totally engaged in my development progress.

I'm part of different personal development structures for me and for you, my client.

So don't hesitate to contact me. You know how to put this into action. You have a clear recipe to do it. I've already given you different options to do it. You have all this inside you; you just need to put it down in black and white.

God only puts in front of you the things that you can solve. You have all the talents inside you. You have all the necessary tools inside you. This process is just a way to get it out, put it in front of you, and discover what you have within yourself.

Take the opportunity to reflect on that. Take the opportunity to provide this tool to your kids and to your future generations. I truly believe people should be learning this in school. They should be learning this before they decide to pick a career. They should be clear about their pathway before asking for a grant or a loan to go to a college or university and have to pay for that loan for many years after that.

People should be clear about their passions and values in all areas of their lives. And it's not too late for anyone to do it. Remember, at age sixty-five, Colonel Harland Sanders began franchising his chicken business KFC.

You are not alone. I'm here to support you. The goal of this book is not only to change your life; it's to improve the lives of everyone that needs this information. And if we do that, we will strengthen our family, our community, and our company. And in the end, we will live in a better world. I'm writing this book not only for you, my reader. I'm writing this book for my kids, for their friends, and for my grandchildren.

I want them to have a real guide in these crazy times that we are living in. So my hope is that you use it and that you share it with the people you love. And in that way, we make a better world.

A big thank you from your inner self and me.

By adopting a positive and proactive attitude to self-awareness, you may create the possibility for improvements in confidence, self-efficacy, and resilience. Of course, it might take a minute or twenty minutes from your day. You can, however, make the fundamental changes you want to make by committing to living in the present moment as your true self and allocating time for your well-being and development. Changes will take you to places you've always wanted to go—mentally, physically, and spiritually.

I'd like to remind you that on my website at www. worklifebalancedoesntwork.com, I've provided a number of free resources so you can continue your self-discovery journey using multiple tools. Please take a look at these free materials.

Thank you for your time. Thank you for your passion. Thank you for allowing me to be part of your dreams and your new reality.

Remember, you are not alone. I'm here to support you. Take some minutes, go to my website and check out my services or other books or courses.

This book is a good start, but it's not the only way. There are many programs I can provide you with. There are many I can create for you, and not only for you but for your community. For example, if you want me to give a presentation in your town, I'm open to doing that. It's part of what I do. I'm a speaker, a writer, a hypnotist, and a trainer in all these things. I can create a full program for your company, and I can teach it to your human resources department. In that way, every person in your company can benefit from this program. In the end, there is the goal. The goal is to impact each person around us in a positive way.

Evaluation Assessment

Step 1: Reflect on your current state. How would YOU evaluate your life in your personal space? Those categories over which you have control and which reflect your **ESSENCE**? You might want to go back to Chapter 6, then place a mark in the box that reflects the score in that category from -4 to 5 of who you are.

Evaluation *Explanation below*	Clinical area		Struggling with life		Struggle	Happy People		Well-being	Magic	ONE with the creation
ERGON Score	-5	-4	-3	-2	-1	1	2	3	4	5
Physical health | Strength										
Intellect | Mind										
Emotions | Heart										
Character										
Spiritual self | Soul										

Step 2: Calculate your essence score by writing each score per category on the table below, adding them all and dividing them by 5; then placing the values in the appropriate boxes.

	Score	
Physical health | Strength		
Intellect | Mind		
Emotions | Heart		
Character		
Spiritual self | Soul		
The Sum of Essence Scores		
Divide the Sum of Essence Scores by 5		This is YOUR ESSENCE Score

Step 3: Reflect on your current state. How would YOU evaluate your life with others, your relationships, and the areas that involve others to make it happen? How would you rate your **WORLD?** You might want to go back to Chapters 7 and 8. When you're ready, place a mark in the box that reflects the score in that category from -5 to 5. Write the score on the column at the right, add all of them, and divide by 5. That is YOUR World Score.

Clinical Area	Struggling with Life	Struggle	Happy People	Well-Being	Magic	ONE with Creation	
	-5	-4	-3	-2	-1	1	2	3	4	5	Score
Love											
Legacy											
Social											
Finances											
Career											
The Sum of World Scores											
Divided the Sum of World Scores by 5											

Step 4: Determine your WEB Score by adding the World Score plus your ESSENCE score and dividing it by 2. This score should reflect your overall life state and will reflect the characteristics in your life shown in the next step.

Step 5: Map the score for every category in the chart below, including your World, Essence, and WEB scores. This will give you a visual understanding of your current life state.

ERGON WEB Bond Assessment Results

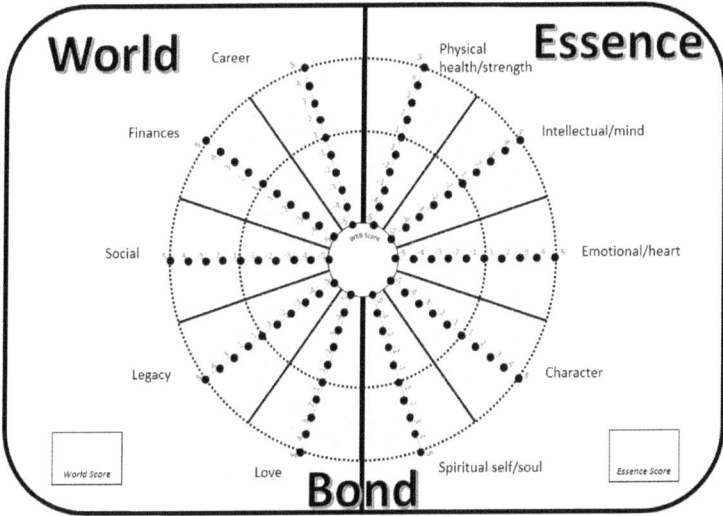

Step 6: Compare and contrast your WEB score with your well-being using the PERMA profile tool. Follow this link and complete the assessment: **https://www.purposeplus.com/survey/ perma-profiler/**

Step 7: Obtain your final assessment overview by circling each score obtained in each evaluation:

	-5	-4	-3	-2	-1	1	2	3	4
	1	2	3	4	5	6	7	8	9
	10	9	8	7	6	5	4	3	2
	Clinical Psychology Area		Struggling with Life		Struggle	Happy People		Biopsychosocial-Spiritual Well-Being	Recrea Your Reality
ics	Professional support is required		Dependable		Dependable	Independent		Inter- dependent	Magic your li

You Are Invited!

Ignacio J. Segovia offers live group coaching on Zoom calls. Reserve your seat in our next group call at:

https://swiy.co/groupcall

Visit worklifebalancedoesntwork.com for dates and locations.

Learn the advanced tactics that can help you attain prosperity and alter your life in many ways.

Book an appointment at

https://swiy.co/calendar